CHAILEY HER

A hundred years

KENSINGTON PALACE

It is a great honour to follow Her Majesty Queen Elizabeth, The Queen Mother as Patron of Chailey Heritage School and this is a particular pleasure in this, its Centenary Year. Her Royal Highness Princess Alice, Duchess of Gloucester, my mother-in-law, also visited the school on a number of occasions in its early years and this is a significant historical link for me, to the role I am delighted to be taking on.

This book is a record of Chailey Heritage School from its foundation by Dame Grace Kimmins in 1903 to the present day. The story is one of invaluable pioneering work undertaken by many dedicated experts and volunteers which still continues today. It will serve as a reminder of times past and be an inspiration to those who follow in the cause of improving the lives of disabled children.

I know that Queen Elizabeth thought very highly of Chailey Heritage School and its remarkable achievements, and at this time of remembering its 100 years of history I greatly look forward to playing a part in its future.

Brigitte

Her Royal Highness The Duchess of Gloucester GCVO

CHAILEY HERITAGE
A hundred years

David Arscott

S.B. Publications

Text © David Arscott

Front cover photograph: 11-year-old James Schueler with his mother, Sandra. [*Daily Mirror*]
Frontispiece: Queen Elizabeth, the Queen Mother, for almost 70 years Patron of Chailey
Heritage, on her last visit in July 1983. [*Courier Newspapers*]
Facing title page: Photograph of the Duchess of Gloucester © Tim Graham
Title page: William Dye, Emma Goldring and Michael Grier posing for Chailey Challenge
brochure pictures outside the chapel. [*Kit Houghton photography*]

ISBN: 1 85770 269 7

British Library Cataloguing-in-Publication Data.
A catalogue record for this book is available from the British Library.

Book design: David Arscott at Pomegranate Press

Published on behalf of the Friends of Chailey Heritage by SB Publications,
19 Grove Road, Seaford, Sussex BN25 1TP

Printed by Pageturn Ltd, East Sussex, BN3 7DX. Tel: (01273) 821500

Foreword

by Baroness Cumberlege
President, Friends of Chailey Heritage

It was one of those dreary days in the Easter holidays with persistent rain. My brothers, rigid with boredom, decided to beat up their younger sister. 'Oh, for goodness' sake,' said my mother, 'get in the car and we'll go to the Heritage.'

This was a familiar treat. After a quick phone call to get permission we piled into the car and drove the short distance to the gym at Chailey Heritage. The remedial gymnasium, sited on the top floor of the Obermer building, seemed fantastic to us. It was well equipped, and we had it to ourselves for as long as we wanted because the Chailey children were on holiday. At my school I hated physical education, as we were forced to do things that I knew my body would not allow. At Chailey it was altogether different, as we could do what we wished. It was fun, and to my mother's delight we returned home exhausted.

My family's association with the Heritage began when I was four years old. My father, Bertie Camm, a local GP, was employed, not to look after the children (he was not a paediatrician), but the staff. He never failed to be impressed by the skill, commitment and compassion of those who worked there. He would give us glimpses of some of the challenges, and we would learn more from the Quibell children, whose father was the medical director, as they were our close friends.

As children we quickly learnt that Chailey was an exceptional place which did remarkable things for children suffering from the consequences of many physical problems including TB. We did not know the full implications of this crippling disease. From the top deck of the 89 bus we looked with wonderment at the balconies upon which, fleetingly, we spied rows of beds with white coverings in which sat children, seemingly motionless. Later our neighbour's son returned from the Heritage – to our eyes a very well adjusted and ordinary little boy, though of course children seldom discuss their past but simply want to fit in with the present.

Later, at 16, I went with my father to the opening of the Memorial Hall and still later to the opening of the Lady Hoare workshops at the New Heritage, which was by now embracing a new challenge of educating children whose future had been jeopardised through the drug Thalidomide. Much later, when I was a government minister, I was asked to meet a group of adults who had been severely disabled through Thalidomide. They were angry and were on a hunger strike. I was asked by the Secretary of State at half an hour's notice to try to persuade them to give up the strike. I was so grateful to Chailey for having taught me a little about this condition, and what to expect, and to have some insight into what these people might be so angry about. I am glad to say they did give up the strike. It was probably not due to my intervention, but it might have had a little influence.

As children we were always conscious of the importance of the Heritage. Not only were there constant reminders through the many people in the surrounding villages who found worthwhile employment caring for children with multiple and complex disabilities. There were the collecting tins on the counters of all the local shops, the coverage in the local press and there were the royal visits. These reinforced our perception of Chailey as a very special place indeed.

I lost touch with Chailey for a time until I was appointed to chair the Brighton Health Authority. It had the day-to-day responsibility of managing the NHS clinical services which supported the school, but the funding came through the regional health authority. It soon became clear that the very future of the NHS facilities were at risk. Times had changed, and questions were being asked by the region about the kind of care Chailey was providing. Was it suitable for the times in which we were now living? Numerous reports were required. We had to produce option appraisals, costings, and the justification for our assessment of future numbers. There seemed little recognition that one of Chailey's great strengths was its ability to be flexible and look to the future, always meeting the changing demands of children and their parents.

When my sister-in-law, a trained nurse, returned from Canada she went to work at the Heritage. She loved the children on her ward, and would bring them home to her house at week-ends and invite them to stay with her in the holidays. She was not unusual in this: like so many staff, she considered Chailey not as an institution but as part of her family.

It is difficult to escape the clutches of Chailey once you have become involved. My reacquaintance with the Heritage certainly had that effect on me. Running through every decision, every new plan, every activity the question is asked: what is best for this child?

Now that I am chairman of the Trustees and president of the Friends, Chailey has once again entered my life and I marvel at the enormous amount of progress that has been made, embracing new technologies, new facilities, new ways of teaching. The quality of children's learning and life has been enhanced far beyond what would have been possible even ten years ago. Chailey has sought to ensure that the children who come to school are not hidden away but go out to meet the world.

The world also comes to Chailey through many routes, not least through its army of committed volunteers. A huge amount of what makes Chailey special has, since the very early days, been undertaken by volunteers. This is not, of course, to diminish the professionalism of the Heritage staff, many of whom, in any case, give of themselves far beyond the call of duty, but this centenary is an opportunity of celebrating the whole community that is Chailey Heritage, past and present.

As the Heritage enters its second century I have no doubt that it will continue to experience change and, sometimes, the kinds of vicissitudes which have threatened its existence in the past. I am equally sure that it will be able to draw on the lessons of its remarkable history in order to retain its position as a centre of excellence at the forefront of education and of caring for children with multiple disabilities.

Introduction

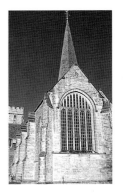

*T*his is a love story, but one that betrays scarcely a trace of sentimentality. It tells how one doughty woman's inspiration became a unique collective enterprise, bringing help and hope to thousands of young people who, in another place and at another time, might easily have found themselves cruelly discarded.

It is, in part, social history. Early references to 'cripples' and to the loneliness of children allowed only fleeting visits from their parents may make us shudder, but they are of their period rather than a reflection on Chailey itself: future generations may very well find our own practices and uses of language disturbing. It is also, in part, a medical history, charting a succession of conditions (rickets, polio, spina bifida, cerebral palsy and so on) and the methods used to treat them. First and foremost, however, it is a testimony to abiding human qualities such as courage, determination and ingenuity (together with a few inevitable failings, too), related as far as possible in the words of the people themselves.

The Heritage began on one site and eventually spread to four before, in recent times, consolidating at its original location: this is often referred to in these pages as the Boys' Heritage or the Old Heritage. The Girls' Heritage was built half a mile away (but a good two miles by road) early in Chailey's history, later becoming known as the New Heritage. On the common across the road from the Old Heritage, was the boys' residential block – the wooden 'Kitchener huts' erected during the first world war giving way to an imposing range of brick buildings, St George's, in the 1930s.

The fourth site was Warren Wood, the nurses home close to the New Heritage which was given in 1948 by Col J.R. Warren, whose family was to have a long involvement with Chailey – his son Michael was later a regular presence as chairman of the house committee. Thanks to generous donations of huge sums and small, the facilities were continually changing and improving at all these locations, and from 1924 until the second world war there was a further site at Tidemills, near Newhaven, housing the Heritage's 'marine annexe'.

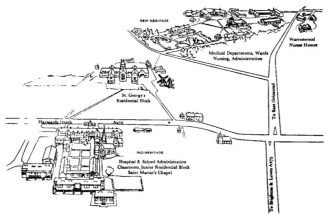

The Heritage on its four sites: the Old Heritage on the A272, St George's residential block on the common, and the New Heritage to the north-east, with Warren Wood close by.

David Norris: a similar photograph appeared on the cover of the 1948 Chailey Heritage book. [Hulton Ltd]

The Chailey archive accumulated haphazardly over the years in a pair of metal cupboards far from the buzz of Heritage life, and it was both a pleasure and something of a challenge to sift through the photographs, scrapbooks, press cuttings and memorabilia amassed largely, although not entirely, during the benign rule of the remarkable Grace Kimmins – the founder of the 'colony' who is occasionally referred to in the text as Commandant (a title she encouraged) and the Dame (as she became shortly before the end of her life).

Mrs Kimmins was responsible for two books which feature at various points in my narrative, The *Coming of Age of the Heritage Craft Schools* – to mark, as the title suggests, the first 21 years – and *Heritage Craft Schools and Hospitals Chailey 1903–1948,* a retrospective of the charity shortly before its absorption into the National Health Service, and usually referred to in my text as 'the 1948 book'. (This was dedicated to Alice Rennie, 'my friend and partner', who is otherwise, regrettably, almost entirely absent from the archives.) I have also drawn on material in *Heritage News* and other Chailey publications, and am indebted to the unpublished account by Howard Ainsley of the work at Chailey from its foundation until 1991.

My appeal through the Heritage and local newspapers for reminiscences about Chailey brought a gratifying response. Memories are fallible, and not all of them are verifiable, but this account would be very much the poorer without the great many stories and reflections offered by former teachers and nurses and, most important of all, by former pupils and patients who lived the experience.

Is Chailey Heritage a school with medical facilities attached or a hospital with a teaching arm? The question would have been answered differently at various times in the past. Suffice it to say that this account attempts to do justice to both the educational and health aspects of the work, without becoming bogged down in the kind of detail that would be of interest only to professionals in the field. Chailey, after all, belongs in a spiritual sense to everyone who has been involved in its century of education and care – to those professionals, certainly, but also to the huge numbers of supporters and volunteers who have given their time and money to the cause.

Most of all, of course, it belongs to the thousands of young people who have passed through the place over the years, and whose voices we hear over and over again in these pages. They are not uncritical (and we should not wish them to be), but their memories collectively are positive and warming. Chailey Heritage has magnificently fulfilled its founder's ambitions – and long may it continue to do so.

David Arscott
Lewes, February 2003

Alice Rennie's own copy of "The Story of a Short Life", signed by her in 1901 and given an embroidered cover.

Brave Poor Things

Nobody reads her today, but the works of Juliana Horatia Ewing were an inspiration to the young Grace Kimmins, the remarkable founder of the Heritage Craft Schools for Cripples in Chailey. One of them in particular, *The Story of a Short Life*, suggested both the name for Mrs Kimmins' first charity, The Guild of the Brave Poor Things, and its Latin motto.

'Irrespective of age, creed, or any other limit,' she was to write later, 'the Guild gathered together all maimed people, whether men, women or children.'

Founded on St Martin's Day, 1894, the Guild had its first meetings in south-east London, but it would eventually have branches throughout the south of England, including Brighton and Hove. That motto, later to be adopted by Chailey, was *Laetus sorte mea* ('Happy in my lot'), and it was displayed on a medal which members wore on a bright scarlet cord or ribbon.

'It was a charity in the real and true sense of the word,' Mrs Kimmins wrote, 'and was founded to supplement already existing charities for afflicted people. Thus, when a society provided a crutch or a high boot, the Guild, with its social meetings, country holidays and general all-roundness, saw that that crutch or high boot was put to the best possible use.'

Miss Ada Vachell, who ran the charity's Bristol branch, has left us a colourful account of Guild meetings, which she refers to as 'red-letter days' for its members. The tone of it may today seem somewhat high-minded, even patronising, but such criticism seems little more than a sneer in view of what was being achieved by these ardent volunteers:

'Outside the room where the Guild was held, long before opening time, a curious pathetic company might be seen waiting. There were blind ones being led; there were lame leaning on stick or crutch; there were many helpless in chairs and perambulators. One lad, whose face seemed to belie his paralysed limbs, had his chair pushed by a blind man, and the two had many a joke over each other's deficiencies.

'At last the doors were opened and in they came. The blind moved timidly with outstretched hands; the tap of crutches was heard, and the twisted and deformed ones limped slowly to seat or corner they had made specially their own. Down the long hall trestle tables were placed; round one, scattered with newspapers and magazines, the men gathered, while the blind clustered round the piano.'

The programme was a mixture of talk, games, newspapers, painting, basket-making, wood-carving, leather work, doll-dressing, military drill and old English singing games. There would generally be a half-hour lecture for the men, and meetings would end with a concert, the roll call, the 'tug-of-war hymn' and prayers.

'All round the walls were hung flags and banners. The Union Jack had a very important place in the affections of the Guild, for, strange and incongruous as it may seem, this unwarlike company considered themselves a regiment of soldiers, and they were proud of their flag as soldiers should be proud.

From 'The Story of a Short Life', about a crippled lad, Leonard:

'I am thinking very hard, Father. Please tell me again what our motto means.'

'Laetus sorte mea – Happy in my lot. What are you puzzling your little brains about?'

'Because I know I know something so like it, and I can't think what! Yes - no! Wait a minute! I've just got it! Yes, I remember now: it was my Wednesday text!'

He opened wide shining eyes and clapped his hands, and his clear voice rang with the added note of triumph, as he cried, "'The lot is fallen unto me in a fair ground. Yea, I have a goodly heritage"'.

Christmas fun at The Guild of the Brave Poor Things. The guest of honour is the Bishop of Southwark.

'"I wish the Guild was every day, I do," broke from more than one member as they limped away. The last crutch had been found; the last Brave Poor Thing had said goodbye. They had gone back to fight in the ranks, in their outer darkness of poverty and dullness and disease.'

'We look round upon the Poor Things on Guild afternoons, at crippled, twisted forms and pain-stamped faces; the setting of their lives rises before one – the poverty-stricken homes, the daily burden of suffering; one lifts one's hand in a smiling salute to one and another who have caught one's eye across the hall; but to the courage and patience and sweetness with which, in so many cases, life is faced, there is another salute, an inward, and we give it with more than respect – even with reverence.'

Grace Kimmins was not someone to sit still. With her friend Alice Rennie she had already formed a satellite to her charity called the Guild of Play, which aimed 'to turn grey streets into gay; to give back to children their chance to be young; to save them from the dragons of environment and heredity', providing them with art, games, dancing and folk singing.

In a gushing preface to 'Songs from the Plays of William Shakespeare with Dances' (as sung and danced by the Bermondsey Guild of Play, with incidental music; written and compiled by Mrs G.T. Kimmins; published by Novello & Co), Professor Israel Gollancz addressed Mrs Kimmins as 'Dear Fairy Godmother of the Guild of Play', adding: 'By your loving might the slums of Bermondsey become woodland-glades, the pinch of poverty no longer smarts, ragged frocks are changed to festal raiment, and the coarseness of mean streets ceases to harm hearts full of the music and song of Shakespeare and Old England.'

We must hope that Mrs Kimmins was able to take this with a hefty pinch of salt. Certainly transforming the East End of London into a sylvan paradise was not challenge enough. Within nine years of founding the Guild, she and Alice were already planning an ambitious offshoot: the great enterprise at Chailey. It had small enough beginnings. Seven boys from the Guild were brought down from London and housed in an old workhouse and industrial buildings on the common. The initial funds, the founder later enjoyed remembering, were a £5 note, with the accounts kept in a penny notebook.

Fund-raising, however, was a Kimmins speciality.

Mrs Ewing on St Martin, patron saint of the Guild and the Heritage: 'He was one of those rare souls to whom the counsels of God are clear, not to the utmost of the times in which he lived, but in advance of those times.'

The Old Heritage in 1903.

The founder, Grace Kimmins, posed at a desk outside the Heritage buildings in 1903.

Grace and Favour

No successful organisation runs effectively without a degree of teamwork, but for 45 years the enterprise at Chailey was inseparable from the drive and personality of its founder. Grace Kimmins was in her early thirties when she founded her 'colony' in Sussex, with one young son (Brian) and another (Anthony) soon to follow. Born in nearby Lewes in May 1870, she was married to the noted educationalist and scientist Dr Charles Kimmins, chief schools inspector of London County Council, and therefore had the latest educational principles at her fingertips.

'Let's face facts,' Anthony was to write many years later. 'Chailey is – or was – a dictatorship, but a dictatorship in its finest sense.'

She was, a reminiscence in the *Lancet* claimed, a spiritual successor of Florence Nightingale: 'She would fight like a tigress, scheme like a Machiavelli, persist like the importunate widow, wheedle, flatter and enslave to attain her end.'

A newspaper reporter recalled meeting her in full fig: 'She was wearing, as always, a mauve frock and a broad white muslin cap, which once prompted a friend to remark to Archbishop William Temple: "Here comes Mrs K. wearing her cope and mitre".'

Elizabeth Walker, who taught at Chailey for 25 years from 1949, recalled her first visit to Chailey.

'Among the people who interviewed me was rather an elderly lady in a somewhat curious dress. Everyone deferred to her and her questions were very much to the point. At the end of the interview she demanded to know if I was strong and healthy. I didn't really understand the reason for this concern at the time, but I know it now. Of course, this was Grace Kimmins.'

Verena Hanbury, Grace Kimmins' granddaughter and currently chairman of the Chailey Heritage School governors, has vivid early memories of her.

'She was a little person with a huge personality. She had this one vivid dream in life which was to create the Heritage Craft Schools. She had arms open wide, a big smile and she adored her grandchildren, but no one came between her and her dream.

'She could have been a suffragette. She went to London and cut her hair short and smoked cigarettes, and she went to work in Bermondsey. That's where she started the Guild of the Brave Poor Things – a meeting place for 'crippled' adults – and it was while she was doing this work that she looked around her and saw that children with these same disabilities were totally uncatered for. They were sitting in the streets with begging bowls, they were suffering from malnutrition, TB bone, rickets – disabilities which today you would probably hardly notice but which at that time were considered to render that individual totally useless.

'She met her husband in Bermondsey and had her two sons. Yes, she adored her family, but the school was her crusade.'

What Grace Kimmins needed was money, and she soon revealed a genius for shamelessly persuading people to part with it. For aggressive

Letter to Mrs Kimmins from Sir Lionel Halsey, St James's Palace, May 23rd 1929, regarding a gift from the Prince of Wales:

'His Royal Highness has just been given the sum of £500 by a friend to be devoted to any deserving case, and he feels that he cannot do better than to send it to rebuild Chailey.

'As his Royal Highness wishes to show his own interest, I am also desired to forward you the enclosed cheque for £25.'

A Son Remembers

Anthony Kimmins, son of the founder, wrote a foreword for the 1948 book on the Heritage, and this is a shortened version:

'My earliest recollection of the Heritage Craft Schools is at the age of seven, when my brother and I were dragged out of class at my preparatory school to answer an urgent telephone call from my mother in Sussex. It was to tell us that the Chailey Parish Council had decided to sell the old tumble-down house (previously rented), the Heritage, and therefore in consequence she could now start planning her Colony for Cripples in real earnest. I wasn't quite sure at the time what it all meant, but one thing will live for ever in my memory . . . the excitement in her voice.

That was in 1909 and since then it has been my good fortune, as her son, and later in life my privilege, as a member of the governing body, and a trustee, to watch the Heritage grow.

Some of the milestones in that growth are described in the following pages, but what is missing is any mention of the excitement and inspiration which carried mother through from one achievement to the next, never looking back, never pausing for breath, but always surging on with but one thought, the welfare of her cripples.

Let's face facts. Chailey is – or was – a dictatorship, but a dictatorship in its finest sense. The present Heritage Craft Schools could never have been built in one lifetime had each vital forward step been fetterered by committee meetings, showing of hands . . . and too much common sense! No, it needed a woman with enormous drive and personality, a resolute knowlege of what she wanted, a tremendous belief in her own powers and – above all – an over-riding inspiration . . . 'The Public School of Crippledom'.

Heaven knows, the beautiful buildings and comforts of the Heritage are a sufficient achievement in themselves, but inside those bricks and slabs of Sussex stone exists something far more important . . . a spirit, which I defy anyone to find the equal of in any other similiar establishment in the world.

Have you heard those children cheer? Have you heard them sing? Have you heard them read the lessons in chapel? Have you shared – no matter how bad their affliction – their smiles? If you haven't you don't know the Heritage, and you have missed something very wonderful.

The Heritage will move with the times. But one thing can never be changed. The spirit of the children who are cured and educated there. Laetus Sorte Mea. That spirit will be passed on from one decade to the next in glowing memory of the woman who not only conceived the brilliant thought of the Heritage, but gave her best years and boundless enthusiasm to its fulfilment.

By far the greatest pride in my life is that that woman happens to be my mother.'

marketing she surely had no peers, and she was ahead of her time in catching the public imagination with a series of ingenious stunts and drives.

'I think she recognised,' says Verena Hanbury, 'that because this was a "first", and because she was dealing with children, and particularly disabled children, there would inevitably be a lot of interest. She tapped in to that, and she became known as "the greatest beggar in England". She had no qualms at all about asking people to support her. She had a great way of involving either very well known or very well off people who she knew could help her cause, and she would get them down to Chailey and she would treat them like royalty, and the children would line up and salute and give three cheers, and they all felt absolutely wonderful and they would sign a big cheque before they left.

Mrs Kimmins with her sons Brian and Anthony.

'She'd wake up every morning, look through the *Times* obituaries, and she would get on the train and go to London and knock on solicitors' doors and say "What about us?" And of course it worked: the legacies were a huge part of the income.'

At first, as we have seen, there was practically nothing. In a letter drafted in 1905, Mrs Kimmins appealed for basics: 'We are badly in need of boys' clothes of all sorts . . . We particularly want Norfolk coats and, indeed, whole suits of any sort, and underclothing, vests, cardigan, jackets and boots for boys of all ages. It is impossible to buy what they really need, for the expense would be too great. Gifts of food, fruit, sweets, books, games etc for Christmas will be greatly appreciated.'

Their needs were soon to be much greater. A visit by His Majesty's Inspectors in July, 1910, produced the following report:

'The school is conducted in two separate departments for boys and girls respectively. The girls are housed in the admirable Llangattock School, completed two years ago, and live under conditions which are most likely to improve their physique as well as to advance their educational and individual progress.

'The boys continue, unfortunately, to use the old workhouse buildings, which leave much to be desired. There is practically no aspect of the accommodation which is not open to serious criticism, and while it was possible in 1904, when the school was first recognised, to accept the buildings as suitable for temporary use, the time has now come for the committee to seriously consider the provision of premises which will satisfy the hygienic requirements of a residential school.'

This report, although damning, was nevertheless somewhat restrained.

'The rats were in sole possession and swarmed everywhere,' Mrs Kimmins was later to recall. 'The beds had to be dragged about when the rain poured in from the leaky roof. There was no gas or electricity, only oil lamps, and no telephone – the nearest public telephone was at Plumpton, five miles away. All water was pumped by hand.'

The education authorities understandably insisted on new buildings if the Heritage was to survive, a demand which surely would have defeated a lesser mortal.

The Black Cat cigarette millionaire Bernhard Baron was a generous benefactor at Chailey, and Olive Fraser, who spent three years as a nurse at the Heritage from 1927–30, remembers one of his visits:

'A highlight was Mr Bernhard Baron's birthday, when he came to the opening of the schoolroom he had given, and the chorus that greeted him:
"Mr Bernhard Baron is 77 today. He's lots and lots of money, and he gives it all away!"'

'How did it happen?' Mrs Kimmins asked rhetorically in a book celebrating the first 45 years. 'Listen! The first large sum – £500 – came from the aged peer, the great and good Lord Llangattock. Then a like sum from the baby daughter of Mr and Mrs Andrew Carnegie – when in long clothes – as a thankoffering for that long-wanted babe. Two pounds came as a legacy from an old one-armed naval pensioner – member of the Guild of the Brave Poor Things. Five thousand pounds from HRH the Princess Louise, Duchess of Argyll, the first Patron of the Colony, who, by a letter in the *Times*, asked, for, and of course received £5,000. Until her death Princess Louise was a most active Royal beggar in the interests of the Heritage.'

The founder was in her element with the great and the good, and she played the royal card with great skill, but she made sure to include the ordinary man, woman and child in her campaigns, too. A little light, but unseemly, fun was had at the expense of Mr Ware, that pensioner who left his mite to the Guild, 'hoping that with such wealth at its disposal it might

At the Savoy dinner, 1935, where the toast was 'The public school of crippledom'. There were little Sussex trug baskets on every table, each containing golden apples with labels conveniently attached on which donors could write their names and addresses.

face the future with no further anxiety about money matters'. The fact is that the Heritage's considerable income derived from many a small contribution such as his in addition to the large sums wrung by Mrs Kimmins from the pockets of the wealthy.

Among the latter was Seymour Obermer.

'He and his wife Nesta lived in Plumpton,' recalls Verena Hanbury. 'They didn't have children of their own, and he always said that he didn't like children. He was walking over the common between the Old Heritage and St George's when he met a group of the Heritage boys. They stopped politely and talked to him, and he was so impressed by them that he said "Where does your founder live?" They showed him, and he knocked on the door and said "What can I do to help?' And she said "Give me a building." And he did! The Obermer building housed the printing schools and the remedial gymnasium where today, after updating as part of the one-site development, you'll find our administration area. It was a lot of money – but he had a lot of money and no children of his own.'

Her projects became ever more ambitious, and yet she seemed never to fail. Typical was the Golden Apple Appeal, which invited sponsors to donate £50 to have an apple hung from a tree outside the school chapel, with lesser contributions meriting a leaf or a mere pip – again allowing a wide range of sympathisers to offer their financial support. (The tree, alas, no longer stands, having succumbed to American Blight in 1969.) This scheme alone raised many thousands of pounds for the St George's residential accommodation (by the windmill on the common) during the 1930s. No small part of her skill was in always having a particular target for her current appeal: the beneficiaries knew where their money was going.

UPON WHICH DAY IN 1930 WILL YOU HANG AN APPLE UPON THE GOLDEN APPLE TREE

In 1932, at a fund-raising dinner at the Savoy Hotel in London, the toast was 'the public school of crippledom' – a soubriquet bestowed on the Heritage by that great editor of the *Times*, Geoffrey Dawson. Proposing 'the Chailey of the future', Nesta Obermer (by then a member of the governing body) said of the children: 'The smiles on their faces are like beacons on a dark night. People who give to Chailey always get more than they give.'

The response was typical: 'As a result of this touching address,' ran a newspaper report, 'Dr Cyril Horsford gave £100 which had been entrusted to him by a grateful patient to devote to some charity. Several others followed his lead, and from the Golden Apple tree which adorned the dining room apples were sold at £50, leaves at £5 and pips at £1.'

The children themselves could be sponsored: in 1921 it cost £25 to act as godfather or godmother to a child for a year, a sum which would also put your name over a cot 'from one Armistice Day to the next', while for £1,000 you could endow a bed in perpetuity.

Mrs Kimmins also had a lucrative knack of using totally unrelated events to promote fund-raising for the Heritage. George V's recovery from serious illness prompted her to launch a Schools Thanksgiving appeal for a £25,000 rebuilding scheme, a letter to the *Times* in June 1929

Another Golden Apple for the tree: Mrs Roberston Lawson, a Heritage governor, hangs an apple to commemorate her mother's 90th birthday. Grace Kimmins was far ahead of her time in devising imaginative fund-raising schemes.

suggesting that 'it would be a noble action, and a fitting thanksgiving, if the schools of this country would join together and fulfil this need'. The Prince of Wales gave the appeal £500 which had been entrusted to him by a friend for a charitable purpose, and threw in £25 of his own. (Proving that it had not lost its promotional skills, the Heritage celebrated the 60th anniversary of this appeal by launching a highly successful Schools of Britain Campaign, backed by the Queen Mother, in 1989.) When, similarly, King George VI recovered from illness, Mrs Kimmins again mounted a thanksgiving appeal, persuading schools to make collections among their pupils – the cash going, of course, not to the monarch (who, to be fair, had no need of it) but to Chailey Heritage. In the Heritage archive are letters from children all over the country, sent to Chailey along with their contributions.

In June 1934, after the chancellor of the exchequer had knocked sixpence off income tax, Mrs Kimmins (still busily fund-raising for St George's) wrote an article in the *Sussex Daily News*:

'The Heritage has hit upon the novel idea of asking people to give the chancellor's gift of 6d off the income tax to Chailey, and if everyone in the county and all lovers of Sussex did this, far more than the necessary £50,000 would be raised in a very easy and rapid manner.'

The children of the Heritage, she said, had written a poem about it, although one suspects the hand of her son, Anthony, who counted writing among his talents and was later to write a fondly remembered Christmas play:

> Sing a Song of Sixpences
> The Chancellor's Birthday Gift
> Let every Sussex Householder
> Respond by Action Swift.

Referring to the reopening of Chailey's windmill the previous year by Princess Alice, Countess of Athlone (*see page 74*), she expressed the hope that she would return 'to play the part of the royal miller and accept sacks of sixpences as grist for the windmill,' adding: 'It is hoped that Princess Elizabeth and Princess Margaret Rose will send little sacks to their great aunt on July 18th.'

Chutzpah, brass neck – call it what you will – this was a trait which served the Heritage splendidly over the decades during which she was in charge. It was displayed in its most outrageous form on the day (as Verena Hanbury relates) that the Bishop of London came down for a major event at Chailey.

'A local woman had been supportive of the Heritage, but she wouldn't sell a piece of land on the common that Grace Kimmins wanted for a new development. Standing up to make a speech in front of the bishop and a large crowd, Mrs Kimmins warmly thanked her for her generous gift of the land – and she couldn't do anything but hand it over!'

From an article by F. Yeats-Brown in the Spectator, November 1930: 'When I was driving across country from the girls' school to the boys' . . . my car became bogged in a muddy lane. Instantly a group of boys who had been kicking a football rushed to my aid. They were cripples. One of them – and not the last – was on two crutches. In a moment the car was surrounded; eager hands were laid on front and rear bumpers, on mudguards, back wheels, everywhere; crooked arms and game legs pushed and pulled, and the car, with me in it, bounced forward as if shot from a catapult. Then the whole gang limped and hobbled after, shouting for joy.

'As for me, my eyes were so dim that I drove into another ditch.'

ERECTED BY
1st Baron Llangattock
IN MEMORY OF HIS SON
THE Hon. Charles Stewart Rolls

MEN MADE HERE

Men Made Here

*F*rom the beginning there was a no-nonsense philosophy at Chailey. Many of the earliest arrivals could literally stand on their own two feet, but even those who couldn't were left in no doubt that they were in large part responsible for their own future.

'They were given as their first job the building of a toy ladder,' Mrs Kimmins recalled many years later. 'No matter how badly crippled, or how crude the result, they always had that ladder in front of them as their first achievement. That ladder was a symbol of the ladder of life. Each rung represented an obstacle which had to be overcome in order to reach the final goal. Some boys carved the school motto on their ladders.

'Many an old Heritage scholar keeps his first crude ladder in the place of honour in his home, and more than one has asked to have it buried with him. He will never reach the top – no-one ever does – but whenever he is up against it, whenever he finds the future black with difficulties, he looks at that ladder and remembers the lower rungs, which at the time seemed insurmountable and yet he somehow managed to overcome. The first writing test in those far away days was: "There is always room at the top".'

What did the Heritage give the children, apart from treatment and training? Mrs Kimmins supplied a list of benefits:

> 1 It shows them their position in relation to others, that they may know their place in the world of people.
> 2 It gives them an opportunity to learn how to get along with others.
> 3 It gives them an opportunity to learn life's values, and thus become round pegs in round holes for the social good.
> 4 It makes the children free of all inferiority complex, or of being left out of the scheme of life.

'A more arduous and yet more successful task would be difficult to conceive than that which was first undertaken at Chailey,' she wrote in the Heritage's *Coming of Age* souvenir in 1924. 'It was to be, not a school for normal children, but a school for the maimed; not a school for the well-nourished, healthy cripple, but a school for the cripple from the poorest homes.

'The material provided seemed the least promising that could be found. The results are not merely health and happiness, but habits of hard work and a high morale. It is a work of charity to supply a pair of crutches or an artificial limb. It is a work of genius to inspire a despairing soul with the courage to live and labour cheerfully in a body crippled almost from birth.'

Hard work was an essential part of the cure: 'Those who teach at these schools,' she wrote, 'have need to be alert at every turn, to rely much upon insight, sympathy and individual enthusiasm. Much tact is required to stir the wish to work, and to take a pride in good work done.

'Sympathy may, and does, help a lame dog over the stile, but magnetic power, keen penetration, amounting at times to positive genius, is required to "detect the robust dog who is shamming in order to save the trouble of jumping".'

Extracts from the St Martin Kalendar, with its improving text for each day of the year:

'If for some of us action cannot mean doing, then remember bearing, too, is action, often its hardest part.'
  W.C. Gannett

'Character is higher than intellect; a great soul will be strong to live, as well as to think.'
  Emerson

'You cannot prevent the birds of sadness from flying over your head, but you may prevent them from stopping to build a nest in your hair.'
  Chinese proverb

'A torn pocket is soon mended, but hard words bruise the heart of a child.'
  Longfellow

ROOM AT THE TOP

From The Cripples Journal vol 1, Chailey, April 1925:

These children must be taught as if they were quite ordinary. Special conditions need not be emphasised. Have stairs to some of the buildings – the world contains many stairs, and steep ones, too. Accustom the children to the use of them while at school. Laugh at their failures – do anything rather than pity or discourage any effort. Their grit and pluck will astonish you. Take at random some of the recent exercises in sign-writing class for one-armed boys:

    There is always room at the top
    From his neck down a man is worth a few shillings a day;
        from his neck up he may be a millionaire
    Health is wealth – be a bank manager
    When you are washing, remember you are the only one
        who cannot see the back of your neck
    It is better to put a fence at the top of the mountain than
        to maintain an ambulance at the bottom

Clearly, then, no slacking was to be allowed at Chailey.

'A cripple in body is very often a cripple in mind,' the resident medical officer, M.C. Wilkinson, wrote in a report on psychological training.

'The "Chailey spirit" pervades every department. This is a spirit of cheerfulness and determination. It is begotten of the realisation by the children of the Heritage that, desperately handicapped as they are in the struggle for existence, they must rely upon their own skill and not upon the sentiment of others to enable them to survive – that they must in consequence struggle desperately hard, and that on the top of it all, they must be invariably cheerful.

'Bitterness and lack of faith are conspicuous by their absence, and cheerfulness and self-confidence take their place. Bone and joint surgery are invaluable up to a point, but the "healing wherewith the Master heals" is required to complete the cure and is dispensed regularly in the school chapel.

'To reinforce the establishment of this spirit, every endeavour is made to encourage and to organise cricket and football. Little encouragement is required. One-armed bowlers and wooden-legged wicket-keepers flourish exceedingly. Stoolball is played equally enthusiastically by the girls. A troop of Girl Guides has been formed and is a great success.'

Chailey boys and girls played against teams from outside, and 'the normal boy who visits the Heritage with the sportsmanlike determination to deal gently with the cripple is probably very disappointed when he is asked to tackle a sturdy youth with iron calipers and a crutch, moving extremely rapidly.' No matter: morale was all.

'There was absolutely no sympathy,' says Verena Hanbury. 'You are what you are and you make the best of it – that was Grace Kimmins' idea.

'That best portion of a good man's life, his little, nameless, unremembered acts of kindness and love.'
Wordsworth

'The habit of looking at the best side of any event is worth far more than a thousand pounds a year.'
Dr Johnson

'Look out for the bright, for the brightest side of things, and keep thy face constantly turned to it.'
Jeremy Bentham

'Power dwells with cheerfulness; hope puts us in a working mood, whilst despair is no muse, and untunes the active powers.'
Emerson

'When we build let it be such work as our descendants will thank us for.'
Ruskin

Confident looking lads at the Heritage in the early years.

Her motto was 'Happy in My Lot', and if a child fell over she wouldn't pick him up. And nor did anybody, unless of course the situation was so serious that they had to.'

Mrs Kimmins was proud to publish a letter sent to her by Helen Keller, celebrated for her remarkable life lecturing throughout the United States and Canada despite being deaf and blind from the age of 19 months.

'It is good to give the unfortunate a living,' she wrote. 'It is still better to raise them to a life worth living.

'It is not so much the infirmity that causes unhappiness as the grief of a useless, dependent existence. The human being who does not use his

Raising themselves to a life worth living: boys in the remedial gymnasium.

limbs, his faculties, is less than human; the man who lacks an arm, or his eyes, but who makes the best of his incomplete self, rises to the highest moral stature of our race.

'The sturdy, kind-hearted British people will surely be prompt to help their brave fellows to do something for themselves. It is the fundamental right of every one to realise himself, however imperfectly, and contribute to the common good, however little. Your schools – and may they increase until there is no need of them – will give to some of our hindered fellows the boon of self-support, a measure of contentment, and, above all, a bond between their lives and the rest of mankind.'

Above the main entrance to the Llangattock School of Carpentry for Crippled Boys (erected by Lord Llangattock in memory of his son, the famous aviator Charles Stuart Rolls) were the words MEN MADE HERE. The sign was painted by an armless boy with his toes, and it was regarded as a symbol of the Chailey spirit.

And women? Girls were admitted to the Heritage in 1908, only five years after the boys, but Mrs Kimmins' exclusive reference to the boys and their ladders reveals a favouritism of which many were all too aware.

'She'd cry "Hello, boys!" when she met a group of us,' remembers Daphne Hewitt, a pupil from 1942–54. 'She'd completely ignore us girls.'

Peter Winstanley, who was there at the same time, would sometimes be taken into her living room at the Old Heritage with a number of other lads.

'Her favourite trick was to ask what was wrong with the dining room set which had been made by some of the boys. We couldn't tell, but it was something like a faulty pattern or one rung short, and she'd say: "Don't you be lazy like that boy". She was good to us – but she actually told us that she had no time for girls.'

'No, she didn't like girls very much,' admits Verena Hanbury. 'She started the school for boys but was persuaded that this was extremely unfair, so she built the Girls' Heritage. It was well apart, because she believed very strongly that disabled boys and disabled girls should not meet. She thought they would produce disabled babies, and she pursued this idea with dramatic strength. They met occasionally in chapel, but this restraint of course resulted in many forbidden meetings on the common.'

At the end of school terms the boys were taken to Newick station and the girls to Sheffield Park, a mile up the track, where they boarded the same train, but in different compartments. Later, as medical facilities improved, even the operating theatres were segregated.

'Commandant was very concerned that we shouldn't mix with, or even go near, the boys,' confirms Hilda Ashcroft, 'and when we attended chapel there on Sunday morning she made sure the girls came out first.

'One day, when the boys followed us a little too soon, she tapped me on the shoulder to hurry me up. Now, with my gammy leg I was quite the wrong person to touch, and I toppled over, taking several other girls with me. No-one was hurt, but it caused quite a commotion, and we and the boys got a lot closer than was usual that time!'

'The boys would reach for their socks after the service in chapel,' Daphne Hewitt recalls, 'and they'd take out combs. Sometimes we would

'The crippled soldiers need to be the bravest of all, for the dead have at least due honour accorded them and rest in peace, and the victors have praise and glory and success to crown them, but most people forget those who have to drag on a maimed life year after year.'
    Edna Lyall

'Courage! the instinct of a child, and the habit of a man, which Socrates shows is not limited to bravery in battle, but includes endurance of pain, or reproach, and that the virtue is, in fact, an unknown or indefinable company.'
    Plato

'A man is sufficient for himself; yet ten men, united in love, were capable of being and of doing what ten thousand singly would fail in.'
    Mazzini

manage to meet by the main gate, but it was all very innocent. We were naive, I suppose.'

'It was more than your life was worth,' Peter Winstanley adds. 'One summer, while we were watching cricket, a couple of women walked past and stopped to talk. We got a hell of a rollicking over that. There were a brother and sister there with polio, and they were allowed to meet only once a year.'

Phoebe Cockram said film shows provided a rare opportunity.

'The girls were in the front, boys at the back. When the lights went out we used to chat the boys up, and we always asked Mr Salmon, the engineer, to cough loudly before he was going to turn the lights up, to give us time to get back to our places.'

Despite her regrettable prejudice, Mrs Kimmins would surely have applauded the spirit of Yvonne Allen, who wrote of her experiences in the Summer 1978 issue of *Heritage News*. Her final rallying cry, after all, is a version of the founder's 'room at the top':

'Ever since I can remember I hated Chailey, the children, the staff and myself. I used to wonder why I was born with short arms and legs and why I had to walk on artificial legs; why I couldn't run, dress myself, ride a bike, climb bars and many other things I couldn't do. All these things used to make me very depressed and this caused me to be horrible and rude to anyone who spoke to me at the time.

'As I got older I had to learn to walk on some artificial legs which were known as 'rockers', because to be able to get around on them we had to rock to and fro continuously. I don't think I disliked them then because I used to imagine I was like everyone else. I can always remember being very dominant towards all the other children that I spent most of my childhood with. I don't think I've ever been the quiet kind, and I have certainly not been the best mannered.

'My home life was great as long as I can remember. Oh, we had our ups and downs, but what family doesn't? As I got older, life seemed to mean a bit more to me; every day that went by life gave me just that little more of something – the only trouble is that I've not found that something yet.

'I'm sixteen now, and I'm independent. I can walk on artificial limbs reasonable distances. I can write, type on a POSM typewriter, dance at discos on my legs and with a bit of luck I shall have my own car and will be driving in about eighteen months time. It's only in this year of my life that I have really had a good relationship with almost everyone I see every day and I know that all the staff who have had anything and everything to do with me have done a lot for me: they've done everything they can or could do for me.

'I am very grateful to every one of them, and would like them to realise that they haven't failed and I shall never forget them as long as I live. For without their faith, patience and loving care I wouldn't be leaving Chailey independent, strong willed and with an ambition of my own to go to college for 'O' levels and then hopefully get a job as a radio actress. I think the most suitable motto for anybody, whether they be able-bodied, handicapped, blind, deaf or dumb, is – "Where there's a will, there's a way".'

Arts and Crafts

*I*n its early years Chailey was first and foremost a craft school, with some basic instruction in the 'three Rs' bolted on but with relatively little in the way of medical care: fresh country air and good food were to be the best remedies for conditions which, though painfully real, generally required no sophisticated hospital treatment.

'Both by carpentry and fine needlework, and by means of other crafts, symmetry and beauty of proportion are learnt alike in the Cripple Schools,' ran a *Coming of Age* paragraph, 'whilst music gives a sense of rhythm.

'From the school gardens children pluck their flowers – draw and paint them in the nature study class – finally applying them to a set design in embroidery or woodwork; thus from the very earliest stages the children become creators, and their craft work is the more interesting because often so original.'

Since Grace Kimmins employed first-class craftsmen as teachers, and since many of the children had the use of all or most of their limbs, items of genuine quality were produced at Chailey: the fittings and furniture of the workshop, the schools, the library and the staffrooms were nearly all made by the boys themselves. The workshops developed gradually, but eventually the boys were occupied in carpentry, printing, bootmaking, leather work, silverwork, printing and bookbinding, while the girls were trained in all the branches of needlework, knitting, weaving, mending and

The Llangattock School of Carpentry at Chailey was the gift of Lord Llangattock in memory of his son, the aviator Charles Stuart Rolls.

'In this workshop,' ran an account in the 1948 book about the Heritage, 'there is a tablet which was subscribed for in pence by the mothers of Wales for presentation to Lady Llangattock, on the tragic death of her son, and was intended for the church at Llangattock, but Lady Llangattock felt that it would be an inspiration to the boys if it was placed in the building which was erected to her son's memory.'

Bootmaking and repairing were among the basic skills boys acquired at the Heritage. [*Woman's Journal*]

'housewifery'. The Housewifery and Domestic Economy School opened in 1910, its girls (most of them members of the Guild of Play in London) 'finally qualifying, as most fitted, for laundrymaids . . . parlourmaids and kitchenmaids.'

'We did all our own mending and darning in weekly sessions,' recalls Hilda Ashcroft, 'and afterwards the clothes were laid out on our beds for inspection. The seniors were taught to embroider and to make ladies' underwear from lovely materials.

'One day the Council Guardian made a visit during an embroidery session and, without thinking, held up a pair of camiknickers for inspection. Our giggling made him realise what he was holding, and he put them down in confusion. Ladies' "smalls" were not something to be exhibited in public then.'

The book published in 1948, telling the Heritage story before its absorption into the National Health Service, gives scarcely a mention of academic achievements, understandably stressing a remarkable success in the world of work.

'The entrance step [of the carpentry school] has been worn away by the crutches and feet of thousands of boys, many of whom are now doing extremely well in the employ of some of England's best known firms. Many have their own flourishing shops, employing in some instances large numbers of employees.'

Employers would come to the Heritage to select a boy at his bench, and he would then be given special training in the kind of work he would be doing when he left at the age of sixteen.

With her usual acumen, Grace Kimmins had secured the interest of influential backers. Sir Ambrose Heal of the famous Heal & Sons furniture chain became the 'godfather' of the carpenters, while the Worshipful Company of Cordwainers fulfilled the same role for the leather and boot shops, donating a lathe and occasional valuable gifts of leather.

The Baynard Press was godfather of the printers, who produced (among

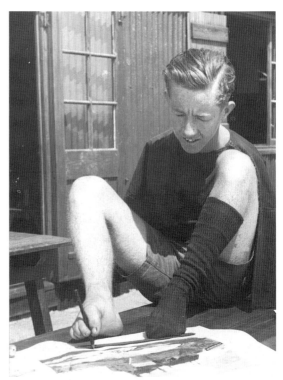

No such word as Can't: a boy learns to paint with his feet.

many other things) the annual St Martin Kalendar, which hung in many homes with an uplifting quotation for every day of the year. (See previous chapter.) Their publications carried the legend, with an appropriate logo, 'Printed on the St George's Press, by the Cripple Boys of the Heritage, at the sign of the Windmill and Pointed Tree, Chailey, Sussex'.

The attractive hand-made items made at the Heritage were sold to raise funds, but they also proved an excellent marketing tool, helping to raise the charity's profile.

'Many famous people – judges, lord mayors of London, university professors, musicians and the like – use the Heritage leather cases,' reads a caption in the 1948 book, 'and many members of the royal family possess (and, we are told, *use*) the suitcases made by the boys in the leather shop.'

All Mrs Kimmins' grandchildren had one (Verena Hanbury still regards hers as a treasured possession), and they of course made wonderful gifts whenever anyone of note came to visit.

The solid oak furniture at the Old Heritage was made by the boys themselves, and 'the benches, tables, forms etc have been most favourably commented upon by trade experts who have seen the work.'

Right: The leather case made for Verena Hanbury – then Verena Elizabeth Anne Kimmins.

Below: George Warner and pupils in the printing shop.

Above: The Bishop of London, Dr A.F. Winnington-Ingram, being fitted with a pair of new boots by boys at Chailey's Tidemills annexe (see page 67).
Below: Royal visitors have been a regular feature of Heritage life – here the Duchess of Gloucester, seen with Mrs Kimmins and the matron, Miss Machel.

Making an Impression

The Heritage archives are a testimony to Mrs Kimmins' enthusiastic seizing of the main chance. There are large scrapbooks full of press cuttings and photograph albums bursting with pictures of visitors (chiefly royals and other people 'of note') being beguiled by the resident children at their most winsome. They would sometimes be measured for shoes, and they would never leave empty-handed.

Who would blame the founder for her courting of the influential? It is unlikely that she fawned over them – she was too much her own woman for that, and once responded to the news that some bigwig or other had been passing Chailey and had just 'popped in' to meet her with the growled response: 'Nobody *pops in* to see me!' She did, however, know how to win hearts and minds.

In 1903, as we have seen, Princess Louise, Duchess of Argyll, was the Heritage's patron. There were, in addition, all of 15 patronesses, including two duchesses, four countesses and seven ladies (one the wife of the generous Lord Llangattock). Another influential supporter from the first was the colony's president, the Bishop of London, Dr. A.F. Winnington-Ingram.

By 1948 the mixture had changed, because the charity was now organised along different lines, but the theme was familiar. The seven vice-presidents included a lady and two knights, while the president was the Duke of Norfolk and the patron was H.M. the Queen: not a bad roll call, all things considered.

The visits were, of course, rehearsed. Margaret Davis (née Bickers) recalled playing her part before the second world war.

'We once had a visit from Queen Mary [1935], and I was also privileged to make a presentation to Dr Winnington-Ingram when I was seven years old. It was a pair of golf socks, and I had to say: "I present you with these socks to keep your feet warm while you play golf".'

There was also an element of subterfuge. Doris Carter was at Chailey in 1936 when the Jubilee block at the New Heritage was opened by the Duke and Duchess of York.

'All the children were issued with new clothes and shoes for the occasion, and I had to learn some words and make a presentation. The girls thought, wrongly, that they would keep the new things after the visit. No, they were all taken off them again after the Duke and Duchess had gone. Mind you, they didn't fit – that wasn't the point of the exercise. I had a blister on my heel afterwards.'

This was not a one-off ruse. The Duchess (later Queen Elizabeth, later still the Queen Mother), came to Chailey on no fewer than six occasions, and Peter Winstanley remembers her 1945 visit with the two young princesses, Elizabeth and Margaret. The boys, who customarily wore a uniform of red highneck jumper, short trousers and a blue smock ('You felt a right twit'), were miraculously dressed in clothes they had never set eyes on before.

Richard King writing in the Tatler, 1921, told of visiting the Heritage and reading to the children illustrated books that had been sent to him for review:

'It made me sad, in spite of the joy they showed in these books – perhaps because of it – to think that all these cripples had come from the darkest corners of the East End; that their little baby eyes had rested on the ugliness and sordidness which is life in Bermondsey and Shoreditch and East Ham. And that here they were living the ideal child life, happy and cared for, while being educated in the best sense of that word, which is, alas! so little really understood.'

In a letter to the local press in July 1922 the Duchess of Norfolk recalled being a guest at the recent Heritage Pageant, confessing she had not before realised the 'great work' being done for the children and wounded servicemen.

'Like all things fraught with real life,' she wrote, 'these schools have come to stay, and I feel that we, as a county, should recognise our responsibility towards them.'

When Jack Hobbs came to play cricket, special turf had been laid by the boys, and he was out first ball, caught behind. The great man suggested, with reason, that the boys would like to see rather more of his batting.

'The umpire gave a tactful "not out", recalled Albert Buckwell, then a gardener at the Heritage. 'It was very bumpy turf.'

'Table cloths were put out, cups and saucers, knives and forks with imitation pearl handles. Different trousers and shirts came out of stock. Even the schoolboys knew that it was a poor show.'

Effective show it was, nonetheless, and certainly many of the children enjoyed these special occasions.

'I remember that when the Duchess of Gloucester got married,' says Phyllis Garrett (née Gane, a pupil from 1929 to 1939), 'some of the senior girls made nighties for her trusseau. They were made of pale blue chiffon, and the bodice was all done in shadowstitch. I can also remember when Queen Mary came. She was a very stern lady, with a walking stick with a silver handle, a long coat, big hat and button-up boots. She never smiled.'

COCKNEY VISITORS

Kath (Dorothy) Crittenden was a pupil at the Heritage in the mid-30s:

'Dame Grace was known and addressed as Commandant – a formidable lady, and we were much in awe of her. We seldom saw her unless escorting VIPS, but she was always very nice and gracious, and genuinely interested in all our doings and our welfare. A visit from her, rare as they were, always bucked us up. A general complaint was that we didn't smile enough!

'I wonder how many of us now remember "A Sunny Smile". This was considered by Commandant to be our school song. The song had quite a catchy tune, but we considered it rather soppy, and it wasn't always sung in the spirit intended.

A sunny smile is worth the while
As you trudge along Life's road.
Though skies be grey, 'twill brighten the day
And lighten the heaviest load.
If now and again the wind and rain
You find a bit of a trial,
Just trudge right on with a cheery song
And tackle your task AND SMILE!

So be of good cheer, ne'er falter not fear
Though rough be the road for a while.
Up hill or down, through country or town,
Trudge bravely on AND SMILE!

'She had us sing it for special visitors, and also when the Guild of the Brave Poor Things came on their annual outing. It became a tradition that we sang this song twice through. The second round 'the poor things' (as we called them) were expected to join in. After their ordeal we served tea and chatted to them – and found their cockney humour quite fascinating and daring!'

'I also remember when the Duchess of York, later the Queen Mum, came. She opened the Black Cat wing, which was an orthopaedic wing. I and another girl dressed up as black cats, and we presented satin purses to her. That was a big day in my life.'

Mrs Kimmins' respect for royalty would sometimes make considerable demands of the staff. A nurse at the Tidemills annexe remembered her reaction to the death of George V in 1936: 'Black diamonds had to be sewn on the sleeve of every boy's weekday jersey, taken off on Saturday night in order to be sewn on to Sunday smocks, and reversed again on Sunday night to school clothes for the whole month of mourning.'

Hilda Ashcroft (née Sherwood) arrived at Chailey in 1923, at the age of thirteen and had a special role to play.

'When I was fifteen and one of the "old girls", matron honoured me with the title of head girl. The job that went with it was keeping eighty girls in good order, neatly dressed, tidy in all things and properly lined-up for lessons and meals. It was also my prerogative and purgatory to make speeches of welcome to visitors and generally represent the school on any formal occasions, sometimes at very short notice. I was none too sure about the last bit, but matron said visitors would be few that year as the then Prince of Wales would be opening a new building at the boys' school soon, and our annual visitors would be going there instead. We would be at the ceremony, too.

The Queen Mother's 1979 visit (her fifth), as reported in Heritage News: 'She must surely know that she has left behind her memories for the children which they will never lose of a glamorous and gracious lady who descended out of the clouds in a bright red royal helicopter to visit them; and memories for the staff of someone who had recharged their batteries.'

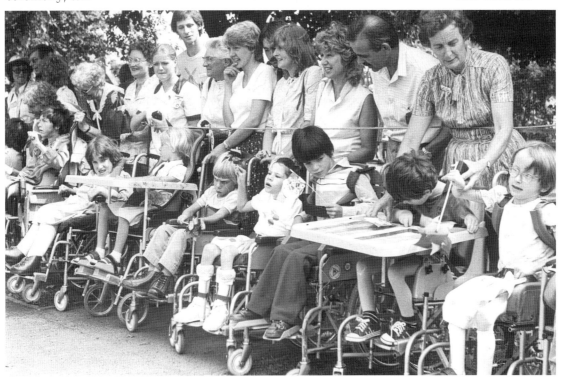

Lined up for a royal visit. Queen Elizabeth the Queen Mother, Chailey's patron, visited the Heritage on no fewer than six occasions, and these children await her in 1983. [Courier Newspapers]

Dr Winnington Ingram, the Bishop of London, was a regular visitor to the Heritage in its early days, and would stay for days at a time. He loved to play stoolball, and wrote in 1933: 'It is the most exhausting game in the world. Every time I score a run 365 cripples shout with joy that an old man of 75 can make a run at all.'

From Heritage News after the Queen Mother's 1979 visit: 'We remember her obvious pleasure in receiving Sue Ellacott's exquisite embroidered tea cosy which would so elegantly set off the butter for the royal slice of bread.'

'In the event, I was deputed to present his highness with a gift after the opening, and to ask him if he might be able to visit the girls' school also. He was a very attractive man, handsome and quite informal, and seemed very interested in us all. One little girl was quite unawed and said "Look, Prince, I cut my finger and had to have iodine on it". He examined it carefully and asked "Well, did you cry?". "Course I didn't," she said proudly. "I'm a big girl." The visit was filmed for the newsreels and I saw it in the cinema during the holidays. There was Hilda Marion Sherwood talking to the future King Edward VIII (even if he was never crowned!)

'As head girl I was kept very busy and was constantly reminded that I was the girls' leader. Sometimes the Commandant would bring in visitors and say, "Hilda, our guests would like to hear the girls sing. Will you start them off, please?", and it was my job to pitch the key and keep them in time.'

Music, after all, was a Grace Kimmins passion.

The visit of the Prince of Wales, later Edward VIII. He is accompanied by Mrs Kimmins and the Heritage mascot, Bowser. [Alfieri Picture Service]

Sweet Singing in the Choir

'The Singing Cripples are famous, and are much in demand for weddings, funerals and so forth, and visitors from far afield are attracted to the services and religious plays which are given from time to time. The choir was the first affiliated to the Royal School of Church Music, and the Heritage boys regularly take part in the festivals.'

So ran a paragraph in the Heritage book of 1948, by which time the colony's musical side was flourishing. The size and prominence of the boys' School Chapel of St Martin surprises most first-time visitors to Chailey, but this was (it should by now go without saying) the result of yet another generous donation. Mrs Harcourt Rose paid for it in memory of her husband. It was built in 1913 of Sussex sandstone, with a red-tiled roof and a lofty spire made of oak shingles.

The chapel was the last church commission undertaken by the ecclesiastical architect J. Comper, who was also to design the residential block at St George's. The nave is all of 76ft long, and the beautiful panelled ceiling of fibrous plaster is decorated in blue and gold leaf with heraldic bosses and carved angels on the cornice. The great west door was the sole unaided work of George Price, one of the first seven boys on crutches.

Richard King, writing in *The Tatler* a few years after it had been opened, described it as beautiful, 'with its regimental flags (some straight from the battlefields in France and Belgium, one of which had been proudly carried before King Albert), its brass candlesticks looted by the Germans from the Belgians and retaken by the Belgians at the end of the war and presented to Chailey, and its stained glass from St Martin's Cathedral, Ypres, in the tiny St Martin's window.'

The chapel, wrote Mrs Kimmins in the 1948 book, 'was a great delight to the late Mr Rudyard Kipling, who was associated with the Heritage from its earliest days, even before it existed save in dreams, and at whose request this lovely shingle spire dominates the landscape in the midst of his beloved Sussex Weald.'

Choristers leaving St Martin's chapel. [Hulton Press Ltd]

Over the years there were many additions. In 1918 Mrs Harcourt Rose gave the Ewing window, as a memorial to the writer who had first inspired Mrs Kimmins – 'an Anglo-American tribute to Mrs Ewing's genius'. The organ was the gift of Miss Violet Wills, in response to an appeal by Bishop Forrest Browne. In 1924 the Douty Song School was built out to the south, an open stone arcade with a large half-timbered room above. This was given in memory of her husband by Mrs Edward Douty (afterwards Mrs Rees Mogg), who also paid for a water tower at the west end of the chapel: this not only held 8,000 gallons of water, but provided a staircase to the song school.

The girls would eventually have their own Chapel of St Helen (another gift) in 1931. Elizabeth Walker, who taught the girls, later recalled the daily routine.

'School always began with service in St Helen's Chapel. I think we all enjoyed this start to the day, but there was a preliminary which I found difficult. Dame Grace liked the girls to have their heads covered in church, so they had to wear chapel caps, rather like unstiffened Dutch bonnets with an elastic band to hold them firm. Many a morning while the majority of the class filed in I struggled to fix a chapel cap securely, pressing it on the top of the head with the palm of my hand while trying to adjust the elastic without the victim suffering a painful snap.'

St Martin's, however, remained the focus of Sunday worship and of the extravaganzas mounted by Grace Kimmins.

'There was a very talented director of music called Mr Leggatt,' says Verena Hanbury, 'and the children in those days were well known for their singing.

'Mrs Kimmins' theatrical side came out a lot in the chapel. For instance, on Ascension Sunday she would give the children balloons as they went out. They would let them go, and they would sail into the sky, reminding them what the Ascension meant. And she had Animal Sunday, on which every single animal under the sun was brought into the chapel.'

On these occasions the chapel was decorated with large, painted wooden animals, and live animals and pets in cages were carried around the chapel during the service.

'We had a donkey called Ina,' remembers Phyllis Garrett, 'and she used to come along too, but someone had to go along behind with a bucket and shovel in case she misbehaved.'

'There was an occasion when the school cart horse was proceeding around the chapel,' remembered C. 'Bomber' Hudson (a pupil from 1942–52), 'when it stopped to relieve itself near the pulpit, which was a huge joke to the pupils.

'Somehow, I am sure by "accident", the horse's harness caught on the lectern, and as the horse started to resume his procession, down came the lectern with a crash.'

Another regular event was the Christmas play, *The Pilgrimage to Bethlehem*. Bomber Hudson had strong memories of this, too.

'The Christmas service was a combination of a Nativity play and service of nine carols and lessons. The chapel was decorated with holly, ivy and

Animal Sunday at the Heritage, when creatures of all sizes were brought into the chapel – whatever the consequences.

Animals also took part in the Nativity play, as Elizabeth Walker (a teacher at Chailey for many years) later recalled.

'One year we had a sheep,' she wrote in Heritage News. 'It was not a natural actress and was much stronger than we were, so keeping it where it should be presented problems. However, one of the girls was a shepherd's daughter and able to soothe and quieten it when all our efforts failed.' [*Keystone*/Brenda Izzard]

A regular chapel event was Noah's Ark Sunday each February. [Alfieri Picture Services]

laurel. The red holly berries, white mistletoe and candles brought the evergreen to life. There were also arrangements of autumn flowers and foliage, together with a dozen or so 10ft Christmas trees. These trees were covered in tiny clear light bulbs, which shone like thousands of stars.

'A manger was discreetly placed to the left of the altar under the choir screen, surrounded by dark Christmas trees covered in stars. Pupils and staff dressed in the costumes of the Nativity characters and assembled in the cloisters around a coke-filled brazier. In the dark, by the light and warmth of the fire, the atmosphere was wonderful.

'As the service of nine carols and lessons progressed, the appropriate Nativity characters proceeded along the aisle to the manger, and as each participant reached the pulpit he turned to the congregation and read the lesson applicable to the part he was portraying.'

Not that everything always went exactly according to plan.

'I played the innkeeper one year,' remembers Hilda Ashcroft, 'and the part called for me to wear a belt with a money-purse hanging from it. I couldn't manage it with only one hand and so it was laid on the crib instead. All went well until the dress rehearsal, when I dropped the purse and disrupted the whole show. Money rolled around everywhere, and one penny ended up right on the toe of an angel whose wings fell off when she bent down to pick it up. Most girls hid their giggles, but I laughed out loud and got a good telling-off from matron, who took everything seriously.'

Mrs Kimmins, not surprisingly, kept a tight rein on her chaplain – as a *Times* reporter once related to his readers:

'In her last years, perhaps concerned over the powers of endurance of her pupils, she would sometimes wave her hand in chapel as a signal to her chaplain that the address should be brought to a close. On my first visit to St Martin's chapel I waited expectantly for this gesture, only to find that the excellent sermon ended without any prompting from the founder.

'Later I learnt that a red light had been installed in the pulpit, operated by a switch which could be pressed from her seat at the back of the church.'

Bernard Trugwell, who was at the Heritage during the second world war with a TB knee, remembers being asked to read the lesson several times in chapel – a building he liked.

'Mrs Kimmins would cow you into doing it,' he recalls. 'You had to practise it during the week, and she'd tell you off in no uncertain manner if you weren't word perfect. She was a bit of a tartar, really. A lot of people were frightened of her, including her own family I should think.'

Tony Williams recalls the founder in her later years, 'a peculiar woman who used to wear a Dutch-style hat with wings and who spoke very loudly. She'd come to chapel sometimes on Sundays, and she'd shush everybody if she caught them talking.'

The Pilgimage To Bethlehem

School Chapel of St. Martin
The Heritage Craft Schools and Hospitals
Chailey, Sussex

Illustrated by
Driver J. B. Archbald, R.A.S.C.
one of the soldiers who was in
The Heritage
Orthopædic War Emergency Hospital

'To take Communion you had to wear this Dutch-shape hat and a big white stiff collar on top of your jumper. It was very, very Victorian, but every Sunday off we would go. We had our best gym slip on and our best jumper.'

Report by Sydney Northcote, director of music, 1927: 'The Douty Singers, being responsible for the music of the chapel services, are a specially trained choir. Besides the ordinary liturgy they perform special anthems at all services. Most of them are readers of music, and music of a fairly high standard is taken. In secular work their responsibilities are similar, and they have a large repertoire of union and part-songs by classical and modern composers.

'Some original creative work is always being attempted, and recently a carol and a setting of a poem (by Henley, the cripple poet), the unaided work of two choristers, were given their first performance.'

The 'Tug-of-war Hymn' was one of those regularly sung in chapel, another being 'The Master Shipwright' – written by Rear-Admiral Ronald A. Hopwood and set to music by Henry Coleman, Mus. Doc, the Heritage's then organist and master of choristers. The first two verses set the tone:

> *The ships in Chailey Dockyard lay crippled as they could be,*
> *Rigging and masts and timbers, and in no wise fit for sea.*
> *And some, tho' new from the cradle, seemed only built to fail,*
> *And none might work to windward in the teeth of a winter gale.*
>
> *So the Shipwrights came to Chailey to succour the ships therein,*
> *For this is the Craftsman's honour to prove what his skill may win:*
> *But gravely they spake and graver, as they saw the halt and lame,*
> *'We must send for the Master Shipwright,' so the Master Shipwright came.*

This hymn was sung at the memorial service of a man who had always requested it on his visits to Chailey, the world-famous orthopaedic surgeon Sir Robert Jones. Sir Robert was chairman and founder of the Heritage's medical board – and he brought, literally, a breath of fresh air to the place.

St Helen's Chapel at the Girls' Heritage. [Stephanie Howe]

Fresh Air and Chilblains

*F*ew memories are more vivid for past pupils of the Heritage than the rigours of a life lived almost entirely in the open air. The discomforts, not surprisingly, feature more prominently than the pleasures, but there are certainly those who speak up for a regime which persisted until relatively recent times.

Michael Baldock's family had a history of displaced hips, and one of his was smashed when he fell off his bike at the age of 14 in 1955.

'It was very cold when I arrived at Chailey,' he says, 'I wore two jumpers, two pairs of trousers and a duffel coat, but these were taken away. After a cold bath, I was given a pair of small blue trunks and had to sleep in a bed outside.

'I immediately went down with a stinking cold, but I was very well after that. I have happy memories of the place. The beds were left outside all year round unless there was a thunderstorm (they were made of metal), and education and everything else went on in the open air, too. I was very sun-tanned – practically black. I was fitter then than at any time in my life.'

This is nothing less than Sir Robert Jones would have expected, but he was something of a revolutionary at the time. At the early, pre-Chailey, stage of his career, he was later to write, his ideas met a good deal of resistance.

'If a child exposed in the open air recovered from its ailments, it was accounted a proof of its "strong constitution", a draught of cold air called for a closed window, and a shower of rain meant a prelude to disaster.

Letter in Heritage News 1979:
'I am enclosing a rather grubby photograph taken in the 1920s of our gym class in the sun costumes we wore all the summer term. This was after the 'revolution', when Mrs Kimmins turned us all into sun worshippers, much to the benefit of our health! Such a radical change caused an uproar among the older staff and senior girls, many of whom left.'

A sunny day at the Heritage – but the children spent most of their time out of doors, day and night, whatever the weather. [*Photopress*]

'A somewhat archaic ritual took place each morning before breakfast. On the count of three we blew into so-called "hankies" (torn-up sheets), after which some luckless girl collected the rejects in an enamel bowl.'

'Hospital committees and even surgeons of renown shrugged their shoulders and buttoned up their coats when they passed through the wards on a frosty morning. This all had to be changed, and the results are now commonplace.'

After Surgeon Commander Murray Levick became the (London based) medical director and heliotherapist in 1923, the efficacy of sunlight was added to that of fresh air. When natural light was insufficient, artificial took its place, and a few years later he published a report charting the success of light, air and diet in treating rickets, malnutrition and polio. The children slept outside (including babies from a few weeks old), but there was a supply of hot water bottles to hand, and the bed covers were made from the same material used by Scott's Antarctic expedition on which Levick had served. He was also to advise on rations for the use of commandos in the second world war, and lived and route-marched with the men to observe the value of his recommended diets.

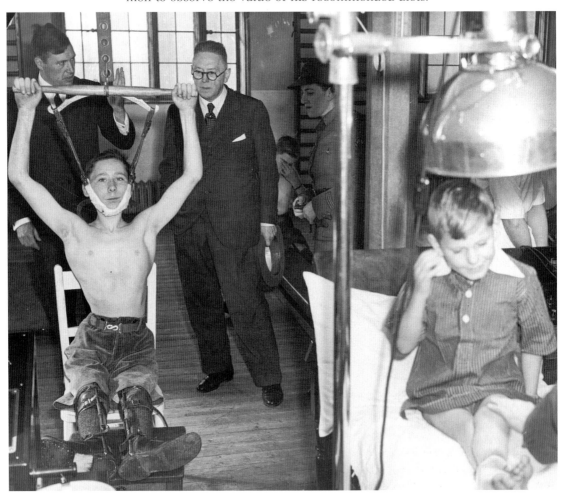

Murray Levick (left, showing guests around) introduced artificial sunlight to the Heritage's range of medical treatments. [Keystone Press Agency]

THE SWISS CONNECTION

Olive Fraser was a nurse at Chailey in the late 1920s:

'Mlle Odette Rollier came to the Heritage at this time as a volunteer worker, and we became great friends. Working with her in the babies' ward on night duty, I actually enjoyed sluicing nappies while she taught me Swiss folk songs and we sang them in unison. The babies treated them as lullabies.

'I can still sing those songs. Years later my husband and I visited the Rollier Clinic in Switzerland, and although Odette too was married, and living in France, her mother was very kind and gave us a great welcome.'

In 1926 the *Town Crier* magazine reported that to listen to the persuasive Murray Levick 'is to gain an entirely new conception of medicine, for he asserts emphatically, and with all the confidence of the man of science, that almost the entire prevention of disease might be brought about by the proper application of light.

'Recent researches in connection with the chemical action of light upon the skin have revealed what civilised man misses by covering himself with unsuitable clothing. And here women, in their recent advance towards greater freedom in their clothes, with their short skirts and low necks, have shown far greater wisdom than men.'

Some four years later *Sunlight* magazine was reporting that, with its natural and artificial light departments, Chailey was comparable to Leysin in Switzerland and was 'one of the most intensely awake, alert, active and ever-accelerated institutions on the face of the earth.'

There were, indeed, contacts between Chailey and Dr Augustus Rollier, whose clinics for surgical tuberculosis in Leysin had opened in 1903, at the same time as the Heritage itself. In 1928 he paid a ten-day visit to the Heritage ('advising, criticising, helping and demonstrating in all departments,' according to the *Coming of Age* book) followed by the sending to Switzerland of those Chailey heads of department who had not yet seen his work at first hand.

The main difference between the two centres, said the *Coming of Age* book, 'would seem to be that Dr Rollier's treatment is carried on almost entirely in bed, whereas at Chailey the new hospital treatment, with its heliotherapy and artificial lamps, is carried on side by side with the experience of the twenty-one years' work in crafts and general education.'

Jean Breech (née Miller) was almost five years old when she came to the Heritage in 1932, suffering from septicaemia.

'Most of the other children had TB hips or spine,' she recalls, 'but I was treated just the same. That meant sleeping outside in practically all weathers. You had chilblains on your face in the winter, and sunburn in the summer if the nurses didn't manage to move you into the shade quickly enough. If you had an infection or a fever you were put in a special shed similar to those you see in Swiss sanitoriums, with an opening to one side.

Sir Jesse Boot gave Chailey £5,000 in 1922, enabling the hospital to be extended, with an operating theatre and facilities for sun and light treatment.

There might have been more. The philanthropist was considering a further donation of £30,000, which would have been used to build six cottages on land already owned by the Heritage and to buy West Field from Chailey Parish Council. Unfortunately his offer met with a somewhat casual response, and he withdrew it.

'I had ultra violet treatment on an elbow, and I remember that they put dark glasses on me for that.'

So successful was the Heritage's sun treatment that Mrs Kimmins floated the idea of opening it to non-residents prepared to pay for it. A leaflet claimed that temporary accommodation would be available 'pending the erection of a special establishment for paying patients of all ages'. These plans came to nothing, but they indicate a growing reputation.

'Picture to yourselves,' Sir Robert Jones wrote of Chailey, 'a group of buildings situated in the most beautiful country and dedicated to the service of the crippled child. You will meet with no heartrending or nerve-racking sight, no agonising incident, but healthy-looking merry children and never a tear. I mean literally what I say, that I have never seen there a child crying. They are hard at work or hard at play, irrepressible in spirit, and yet fully disciplined.

'The spirit of Chailey is not spartan, but there is no maudlin sentimentality encouraged. The child's deformities and disabilities are rarely alluded to. He is filled with emulation and a desire to excel. If he has lost an arm, or leg, he still has one or the other so trained as to minimise disability. It is a perfect joy to see a one-legged boy run a race, and the pride of a one-armed boy, when he shows you what the remaining one has

Fresh air for toddlers at the New Heritage.

46

A great many postcards were produced featuring the Heritage. This one was captioned 'Llangattock School of Arts and Crafts for Crippled Girls'.

From the report 'Care of the Crippled Child': 'The Heritage Craft Schools are situated on the Wealden heights of Sussex, on the subsoil known as the Hastings Sands. They have an altitude of 300ft above sea level. The prevailing winds are from the south west; the rainfall per annum is less than the average for Great Britain.

'The amount of sunshine, always above the normal, is above the average for any other district of England for every month of the year except January and February, when the eastern district is thus pre-eminent.

'The climate is dry and bracing. The air is especially pure. Twelve miles to the south is the sea, and from over it come the prevailing breezes, tempered by their passage across the Downs.'

accomplished. Every boy and every girl fully realise that they are to be of service in the world. There are no drones at Chailey! See them at work in the carpenter's shop or in other industrial developments, and you will realise the happiness of it . . . They are taught the joy and morality of work!'

Many would have taken issue with the spartan comment – among them, no doubt, the little charges of Elizabeth Walker: 'Some girls with TB bone conditions slept in open-sided wooden sheds, and it was disputed whether this was a privilege or a penance. Some of the girls revelled in the freedom of a little wooden hut to themselves, while others found it frightening, especially as there was an owl colony in the wood across the road and the night noises could be very eerie. On winter nights, too, the hut girls envied the dormitory girls, for they often woke with frost on the burberry which covered the bed clothes.'

'Most nights we slept out of doors,' agrees Phyllis Garrett. 'Our heads were always under an awning, but it was nothing to wake up in winter and find snow on the end of your bed. You used to have a fitted tarpaulin that went half way over your bed so the top of you was always dry. No matter how cold it was you had to sleep outside if possible. They said it was healthy.'

'I had terrible frostbite,' recalls Doris Carter, 'from my shoulders to my wrists. My arms had to be covered with bandages and paste, and when my parents visited they thought I'd been in a fire. The tarpaulin didn't cover the pillow, of course, so that got soaked with the dew. It meant that you had to keep your head still. If you turned it, you'd get wet.'

Karen Smith worked as a staff nurse and then ward sister for more than 30 years from the late 1960s, and she took the view that life in the open air was better suited to some conditions than others.

'Youngsters with cerebral palsy just froze,' she says, 'and they suffered from chilblains. It was a problem for physiotherapists, because they couldn't work with cold children.'

Dr C.W. Saleeby, chairman of the Sunlight League:

'Why not try to conquer rickets and "surgical" tuberculosis – falsely so-called – and that ignorance which Shakespeare said was the only darkness, by means of sun balconies and schools in the sun in Sussex? – yes, in "sleepy Sussex", which is indeed at this hour the home of one of the most intensely awake, alert, active and ever-accelerated institutions on the face of the earth.'

Jane Edmonds' family had been instrumental in providing a playing field for the school, and she and her twin sister were christened in the chapel. In 1955 she returned for a 17-months stint as a pre-nursing student.

'I began working on the babies' ward. This was the most spartan place of its kind one could imagine. It was little more than a solarium, open to the elements on its long south-facing side, with a few enclosed rooms on one end. When it rained or snowed, long tarpaulin blinds could be pulled down between the pillars to give a modicum of protection. There was, however, no protection against intruders, who could have gone anywhere they pleased.

'That first winter I moved on to the toddlers' ward, a misnomer really as the children ranged in age from about $2\frac{1}{2}$ to 7 or 8 years. It was under the care of a lovely Welsh lady, Sister May. This ward was much bigger and actually enclosed, with glass doors. However, work, play and sleep still took place outside, day and night.'

The Princess Elizabeth Clinic (PEC) was, according to Mary Sheppard who nursed there, considered to be the coldest place in the Heritage.

'I remember ward rounds taking a whole morning, and by the time we were finished my feet and hands had no feeling in them in spite of a cardigan and fur boots.'

The heat could be a problem, too.

'On sunny days,' she adds, 'the only shade came from coloured umbrellas, one between two cots, and a high green cover fixed to the back of the cot to cast a shadow.'

Doreen Quibell (née Roake), came to Chailey as a staff nurse in 1948, and was later to marry the chief medical officer, Philip Quibell.

'It was a very isolated community – very quiet,' she later recalled. 'I remember that at night it was so dark, the only lights you could see were from the radio mast in Ashdown Forest or the stars. The staff lived in local communities like Scaynes Hill or Haywards Heath, and the nurses lived in the nurses' homes. We were snowed up in winter quite often and the stoker, who lived in Haywards Heath, used to walk in to Chailey in time to stoke the boilers for the morning rush.

'All the children slept outside. Sun lotion-like calamine protected the skin and looked like war paint. In winter we went round with horrible cod liver oil cream anointing hands, faces and ears to prevent chilblains. QEB was for toddlers with a nursery teacher. Babies were on PEC. In the early days this was not a closed building. It was a curved, open pavilion with pillars along the front and a wooden floor.

'The cots were arranged on the curve on the patio outside. If it rained they went under the roof. If the wind beat the weather in, tarpaulin blinds were hung between the pillars. It was a draughty place then, and the babies were well wrapped up and kept warm. But for most of the time bathing, eating and sleeping were outside. Water had to be carried in a bucket to fill a bath on a stand, and emptied down the drain afterwards. It was hard on the nurses' backs.

'PEC was closed in with glass doors in the 1950s when Miss Louise Barnard was matron. Nursing was still out of doors, but the type of patient was changing and the fresh air treatment gave way to antibiotics and better drugs of all types, including immunisations.

'The outdoors regime was particularly aimed at the children with TB. There were children who had chest TB, as well as TB of the bones and joints, and some children with bronchiectasis from whooping cough or measles or cystic fibrosis (which was only being described in the 1960s). These children were nursed on a hinged wooden contraption, which was placed under the mattress and made a hump in the bed, so that the child was lying in a head down/bottom up position for chest drainage.

'I remember that their feet got very cold, so that we had to go round and change the hot water bottles every two to four hours. The babies used to be swaddled in blankets: they were like cocoons.'

'Hot water bottles weren't permitted, so our evening wash often included our feet as well, just to keep them warm. The cold was said to keep us healthy – I think the germs probably froze to death!'

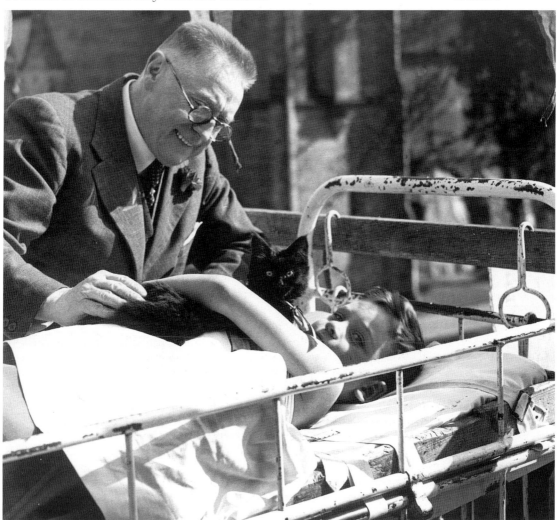

Gilbert Carr, an American visitor, meets a Heritage pupil and friend. [Keystone Press Agency]

This Bruce Bairnsfather sketch appeared in the Heritage booklet 'Soldier Students: A Scheme of Educative Convalescence for the Wounded'. The caption read: 'You and your buck, me lad, are the best pair of crutches for me.'

A Great War

Nothing better demonstrates Grace Kimmins' drive and originality than her response to the terrible carnage of the first world war. It would have been easy to turn her back on events over which she had no control and to concentrate simply on making life better for the youngsters in her charge. That was not her way. Rather, she swiftly opened the Heritage to hundreds of wounded soldiers and 'raid-shock' children. Chailey, in short, had 'a good war'.

'As her war work,' Verena Hanbury explains, 'she gave one of the buildings on the old Heritage site – a building where the boys lived – to the Ministry of Defence as a hospital building, and they used it for young lads coming back from France who needed amputations.'

And then a piece of pure Kimmins 'theatre':

'They would have their operation and when they came round from their anaesthetic they would find a small boy by their bedside who had *never* had the limb they had lost. And they worked together. The chap learned a trade, because that's what the boy was doing. The boy had a hero and the soldier had a friend. He couldn't let himself down faced with that!'

Princess Louise, sponsoring an appeal for £5,000, wrote a letter to the *Times* which was so successful that the Heritage's own funds were left untouched in meeting the costs involved in building the wards for what became the Princess Louise Military Hospital. But if they gave up their own building to the soldiers, where were the boys to live? Simple: they built a series of wooden hutments themselves close to Chailey windmill, with (another stroke of PR genius) an armless boy officially declared clerk of the works. These were the Kitchener Huts, and Lord Kitchener himself presented the boys with their first Union Jack.

There was some delay in building them because of problems over purchasing the necessary land. The money was in place, but 'as so often happens,' Grace Kimmins commented tartly, 'whenever cripples find a home, one or two among their more fortunate neighbours are always found to object to the spectacle in their midst, and to any growth of the work'.

A booklet concerning the 'educative convalescence for the wounded' was published in May 1916, the Rt Rev

Building the Kitchener Huts.

From the Coming of Age book: 'In the Princess Louise Special Military Surgical Hospital, the wounded soldier-student not only received cure and convalescence, but was also taught a trade or craft: and above all, he recovered hope and happiness as well as health. The special pre-war experience gained from many years' work with crippled children was put at the service of the crippled soldier.'

'It would have been hard indeed to find a more inspiring sight than that of the brown-faced eager boys, sawing and planing and hammering in the interests of their soldier guests. Finally, on a bright June day... the central log was declared "well and truly laid" by the vice-chancellor of the University of London.'

From 'Punch'
magazine, 1918:
'Mr Punch has
already pleaded
for the little
children who have
suffered from air-
raid shock and
are being cared
for at St Nicholas'
Home, Chailey,
and he takes no
shame to plead
again. For, though
the Hun was
scared from our
English skies a
long time ago and
is not likely to
return, some of
these children still
need to be gently
nursed and made
strong in the kind
Sussex air.

'Mr Punch begs
his kind friends of
their charity to
send gifts in aid to
the Founder and
Hon. Secretary of
the Guild, Mrs
C.W. Kimmins.'

Bishop Forrest Browne, in a foreword, explaining that 'a batch of sorely crippled soldiers' had been brought to Chailey.

'To each was assigned as orderlies two of the trained crippled boys suffering from the same loss of limb. The boys became the soldier's nurses and instructors. He learned from watching them how to get on as well as they did without a right arm or whatever it might be.

'One man had lost both legs. The Home had only one little boy in like case, and it was delightful to see how the crippled soldier learned from the crippled child as he got about most cleverly on two tiny little wooden legs.

'When convalescence was established, the solders were led by curiosity to follow their orderlies to the workshops and watch them at work. Not at all keen to do anything but laze, they found the nimbleness and the skill of the carpenters and metal workers and basket makers and what-not very catching. Before they quite knew what was happening they had caught the way of the thing, and to their own surprise they were useful workmen.'

The boys in their blue smocks and the soldiers in their hospital blues would often be seen playing football together on Chailey Common, many of them chasing the ball on crutches. Some of the men made small book-shelves for themselves and toys for their children, while one actually fashioned a cradle for his baby, who was born while he was in the hospital. Many of them left Chailey wearing boots and shoes they had made there, having learned the trade from scratch.

'The crippled guests were matched to their crippled hosts,' explained Mrs Kimmins in the 1948 book, 'a one-armed man to a one-armed boy, and so forth: an experiment in psychology of immense interest to all educationalists.

'Typical of the friendship which sprang up between the wounded soldiers and the crippled boys is the story of the gypsies' baby. A soldier in his walks abroad found some gypsies had set up their caravans not far distant from the Heritage, and that a mother was greatly distressed because of the illness of her baby. He at once told the boys' matron, who promptly went down to investigate, and the result was that the mother and child were soon temporarily housed in a detached hut at the boys' Heritage, but after days of anxious nursing the baby died.

'Great was the distress of soldiers and boys alike. The tiny coffin was made by them in the workshop, and the senior boys, with the soldiers, attended the funeral. Old clothes were unearthed from matron's cupboard to make the chief mourners look as respectable as possible, and after the funeral the men and boys escorted the heartbroken couple back to their temporary home, after extracting from them a promise to come and say goodbye before once more taking to the road.

'A collection was then made, and when the couple came they found in the Heritage drive a handsome new handcart, complete with all the paraphernalia of pots, pans, brooms, brushes, clothes pegs, and all the things that go to make up a gypsy's outfit, and seated on the top of this weird collection was my younger son, Anthony, with my elder son, Brian, holding on to the handles, surrounded by the crippled boys and soldiers. The gratitude and joy of the gypsies was unbounded, and this incident is just typical of the Heritage sympathy for anyone in distress. Off went the gypsy and his wife, cheered by everyone until out of sight.'

The St Nicholas Home for Raid-Shock Children (a leased house with grounds near the Heritage) was established in 1917, and youngsters recuperated here until 1920: 'We are too apt to forget,' Mrs Kimmins wrote, 'that for every child that has been killed by a bomb, many scores have been wrecked in mind; for every child that has had a limb blown off, many hundreds have been driven temporarily mad or imbecile with shock. From such bruises the young brain may never recover if neglected.'

The venture was maintained by the *Evening Standard* and Lord Riddell who, helping to raise funds for the venture, expressed the hope that it would be unofficially known as 'the House of Smiles'. In all 590 children were treated, and archive photographs do, indeed, show them with smiling faces – playing games and digging in the garden with the injured soldiers.

Since Mrs Kimmins was canny at choosing appropriate dates for her ventures (the raid-shock children's home was opened on Trafalgar Day),

From the Times, April 29, 1924: 'Chailey actually gave fighting men to England . . . Chailey gave to England, too, something of the spirit of her brave boys and girls.'

Wounded first world war soldiers arriving at the Heritage in style. [Brenda Izzard]

From the Coming of Age book:

'The Great War, and with it, in the hope of all, all wars between man and man, came to an end at the eleventh hour of the eleventh day of the eleventh month. Few noted, however, that the day on which the final armistice was signed was the day consecrated to St Martin, the soldier saint.

'The story of St Martin is surely not yet forgotten. He lives, not for his military prowess, but for his chivalry. It was he who with his sword cut his martial cloak in two and shared it with the shivering beggar. What nobler way of celebrating victory?'

she must have been delighted beyond measure that Armistice Day was November 11 – the very day of the Heritage's patron saint, St Martin. She instigated the 'Roads of Remembrance' commemoration, planting trees given by the leading boys' public schools in England throughout the country each armistice day. Launching it at the House of Commons, Sir Ernest Wild referred to the very first planting – by soldiers and children at the Heritage.

'Included in the programme were the following: Kipling's "Land of Our Birth", the National Anthem, a special Te Deum, a blessing by the bishop of the trees ranged before the altar, the Last Post, later the Reveille and, as anthem, Blake's lines:

> *Nor shall my sword rest in my hand*
> *Till I have built Jerusalem*
> *In England's green and pleasant land.*

'Then "Land of Hope and Glory" as recessional, during which the soldiers, attended by crippled boys bearing flags, carried the trees from the chancel to the road place for planting.

'Whilst the planting proceeded under skilled guidance, tree-planting songs were sung, an interlude being marked by a dedicatory address concerning the achievements of the men commemorated.'

The war memorial remembers 28 former Chailey boys who were killed during the first world war. [Alfieri Picture Service]

The war had proved no distant rumour to the Heritage. Not only had the injured soldiers and raid-shock children proved a constant reminder, but dozens of the boys treated at Chailey had recovered sufficiently to be sent abroad to fight for their country.

No fewer than 28 of them died on a foreign field and were later honoured by the same number of trees planted in that Chailey 'road of remembrance', a war memorial in the grounds (designed and sculptured by Princess Louise) and a tablet in the chapel.

Medical Advance

*T*he Heritage had had a hospital from the beginning, but in effect it was little more than a school sick bay, with no permanent medical staff. Doctors, dentists, surgeons and anaesthetists, chiefly London-based, would make monthly visits. Nature was the great healer.

The transfer to Chailey, in 1920, of crippled boys from the Dartmouth Home in Blackheath, London, marked a major change in the role of the Heritage. Although Grace Kimmins would officially change the name of her colony to The Heritage Craft Schools in 1925 (feeling free to use other titles, such as the Heritage Orthopaedic and Sun Cure Hospital, when it suited her purpose), Chailey was now no longer first and foremost a school with basic medical support. Hospital care would now be as important as schooling, pupils becoming patients. In 1922 a donation from Sir Jesse Boot provided improved medical and surgical facilities, including an operating theatre, in the boys' hospital.

'The medical side gradually evolved,' explains Verena Hanbury. 'Grace Kimmins was encouraged to get the medical side going, and because orthopaedic surgery was a large part of the medical input the children were hospitalised for many months. The school went on as usual, but the classrooms for some were hospital wards.

'As time went by the needs of the children changed. A succession of new conditions arose, and gradually the need for bed rest was replaced by wheelchairs. It was a matter of medical science moving on, really, and of the children having different needs. In the beginning there was malnutrition, rickets, TB bone and that kind of thing, and then you went to polio and on through a succession of new conditions.'

We have some interesting snapshots of this period by way of three reviews published in 1927.

Percy Sykes, the first master appointed in 1903, was still working at Chailey all these years later. His report revealed that most of the 'physically defective' boys and girls were between ten and fifteen years old, and that the majority (a hundred of the 160 boys) could walk the journey across the open common to school twice daily 'with the aid of pole, crutch or artificial limb'.

The rising bell went at 7 o'clock, and the school day ran from 9.30 until 4.30 with a break for the midday meal. Lights out in the evening was, for some reason, staggered along gender lines: 8 o'clock for the girls and 8.30 for the boys.

The curriculum embodied a distinctly vocational bias. On several occasions Sykes had been able to record 'No old scholar at present unemployed', and even in the difficult economic post-war conditions the percentage of unemployment had been very low. Even those in bed could do useful work, the 'bed craft' for the youngest being cane weaving, and for older boys jewellery, silver smithing and metal work.

'The dignity of absorbing occupation, of "employability", is the only real compensation to the crippled. This, coupled with a wide appreciation of

From the 1927 report by Chailey's first master, Percy Sykes:

'From small beginnings in 1903, 23 years of concentrated study, enthusiasm, drastic determination and resolution have produced many unusual features and ideas that have now a tested support and value.

'The lack [hitherto] of companionable rivalry, or the frustration of even spasmodic voluntary tuition, has left little natural anxiety, or grip of future problems to be faced by a prospective scholar. This also applies, in many cases, to his well intentioned and kindly parents.

'Admitted, carefully examined, watched and dieted, the new scholar is now placed in one of many groups, expected to carry out the regular courses, subjects and hours allotted.'

art, literature and music, provides unending opportunities for a full and happy life.'

Sykes was very keen on the public school ethos, even to the extent of having a 'house' system as at Eton and the rest.

'The distinctive advantages of a public boarding school, enrolling scholars from a score of English and Welsh districts – claiming and using public school ideals and methods – whilst providing against helplessness or disregard of life's economic problems, are a commendable combination.'

Sydney Northcote, B. Mus. Oxon, was director of music at Chailey, and he set out the three chief aims of teaching music: psychology, therapeutics and art. He reported that the Heritage had a two-manual organ in the chapel and a specially trained choir which performed in the Douty Song School.

'Many a shy, timid spirit has found a new power of assertiveness and self-expression through the medium of a jolly school sing-song – surely a subconscious curative not to be despised.'

Music was used as vocal therapy, with each singing lesson preceded by instruction in breathing and 'vocal hygiene'. During the summer months music and movement was conducted in the open air, finding 'a jolly harmony in the brown and naked bodies at the classes on the solarium'. It was found that slight facial paralysis or habitual contortion could be corrected by articulatory exercises, and a tendency to stammer could be arrested, too.

Northcote's ambition, and the ability of the 'scholars' to achieve it, can be seen from his account of the Beethoven Centenary Festival held at the Heritage in 1926. Music was used as part of 'co-ordinated education', involving literature, maths, elocution and religious training.

'A lecture on the composer's life and work was followed by a discussion of the general history of the period. By means of dictation some concise notes were taken. Essays were written, the literature and art of the time discussed, some contemporary poetry was prepared for the elocution class and the week's work ended, as it had begun, with an organ recital in school chapel, the programme of which consisted entirely of works by Beethoven and his contemporaries.

'Over and over again this idea has borne remarkable fruit. It is not surprising that early spelling lessons become an interesting game played on the Great Stave, or that early arithmetical experiments have a new fascination when crochets and quavers take the place of figures – and many an interesting tune has been evolved this way.'

The resident medical officer at this time was M.C. Wilkinson (under the directorship of Murray Levick), and his report was the most detailed of the three. Entitled *The Care of the Crippled Child*, it began with a survey of the climate and soil conditions at Chailey (very healthy), and added that the Heritage water was drawn from wells. Each hospital had an operating theatre, a light room, a plaster room, a ward and a large verandah used as a solarium. The girls already had a remedial gymnasium, and a new one was under way for the boys in a building which would also contain a light room and plunges.

Healthy exercise was an important part of the daily routine at the Heritage.

From the 1927 report by the medical officer: 'At a hospital school for crippled children, operation is required to correct deformities and to stabilise limbs. Electrical treatment, massage and remedial exercises are required to restore function. Heliotherapy and general measures are required to build up the patient's resistance to disease.

'As in all schools, periodic dental and ophthalmic inspection are also required. Special attention is paid to hygiene – and, in addition, the atmosphere and environment at the Heritage Craft Schools is generally psychotherapeutic.'

There were 212 children in his care, most having 'types of common chronic orthopaedic conditions': he listed congenital club foot, chronic osteomyelitis, joint tuberculosis, spinal tuberculosis, infantile paralysis and spastic paralysis.

During the winter artificial sunlight replaced the real sunlight treatment. In May 1924 the *Daily Telegraph*, in a glowing report on the Heritage, had lamented the fact that the two operating theatres were closed: 'They are still awaiting equipment. It is a great drawback that at present operation cases have to be sent to the hospitals in London or Brighton, and returned. The children fear the change, the transference from familiar, kindly nurses and doctors whom they know to others, equally kind no doubt, but still strangers. It is to them a disturbing adventure.'

By the time of the Wilkinson report, however, the surgical wards were busy, and between May 1925 and December 1926 some 132 operations had been performed. The children, Wilkinson wrote, had been sent to Chailey primarily to be educated, but 'a cripple in body is very often a cripple in mind.' He used his report to make a powerful medical and educational case for the necessity of treating the children at a hospital school. They had all, he wrote, received previous treatment as some other hospital or institution – and in very many cases deformities had been allowed to develop afterwards.

'One case in particular will illustrate this point. A boy had an attack of encephalitis lethargica two years before his admission to the Heritage. He was discharged from hospital without having recovered the use of his legs. On his arrival at the Heritage he was still quite unable to walk or to leave his bed. On examination the paralysis was found to be purely functional. All the muscles of his legs had recovered and were in excellent condition.

'Minor maladies are infrequent. As many children have paralysed limbs with a poor circulation, special measures against chilblains are necessary. Bathing in hot water twice a day and subsequent rubbing with a dry towel prevents stagnation of the blood and is used as a preventive measure.'

'With suitable treatment, the boy was soon able to walk normally. If this boy had been sent to a hospital school soon after his acute illness there would not have been two years' delay before the treatment required for a complete cure could be given.'

Many of the children, he went on, needed treatment over a long period – all but twelve of the 96 cases of infantile paralysis at Chailey, for instance – and it was far better for them to have their operations and treatment at the same place. The London hospitals were too busy for this: 'the turnover of cases is too rapid and the waiting lists are too long for any one patient to receive more than a due share of treatment'. In addition, the long journeys to and from hospital, sometimes several times a week, were a handicap as regards the children's education.

Wilkinson's report covered physiotherapy, plaster work, heliotherapy, ophthalmic and dental treatment, and gave a breakdown of the 76 operations carried out at Chailey during 1926. Most (41) were for infantile paralysis, with another 14 for spastic paralysis. The others were tuberculosis of the hip (7), congenital club foot (6), tuberculosis of the knee (2), a graft for old osteomyelitis (2), tuberculosis of the elbow, hammer toes, old fracture of the leg and knock knee (one each).

A lesson in the open air with the chaplain, Rev. Fernley Parkhouse. [*M.C.Photos*]

As for 'general hygiene', the chief need was to promote good habits, so that the child would continue with them later in life, and 'if slovenly domestic conditions are then encountered, relapse into poor health is less probable'. In the boys' quarters the wooden floors were swilled down with a weak solution of Condy's Fluid twice a week, and the windows were always kept open. The girls' Montessori school held its lessons in the open air as often as possible, and all the younger girls slept out of doors every night.

'At the Kitchener Heritage, during the past nine years, there have been three single cases of measles, scarlet fever and mumps. In no case did the infection spread to any other child. There have been epidemics of diphtheria: one of these was virulent and spread; in the other only one case developed, apart from a few carriers who were isolated and treated. During the past year at the girls' heritage there have been three single cases of chicken pox, whooping cough and mumps, with no further spread to any other case.'

'As many children have paralysed limbs with a poor circulation, special measures against chilblains are necessary. Bathing in hot water twice a day and subsequent rubbing with a dry towel prevents stagnation of the blood and is used as a preventive measure. The children massage their paralysed limbs in bed every evening, and two pairs of woollen stockings are worn over such legs in winter.'

The boys' toothbrushes were boiled once a week and then dipped into strong permanganate solution to keep them aseptic: a mixture of salt and camphorated chalk was used as toothpaste. Each girl's comb was inspected every day, while the boys' hair brushes were kept permanently in weak lysol: no case of ringworm or any scalp infection had occurred in nine years. No hats or caps were worn, and every girl had her hair bobbed.

In the winter the boys wore thick flannel shirts, woollen jerseys, stockings and linen smocks, with flannel waistcoats added on cold days. (And each wore flannel pyjamas and had no fewer than six blankets on his bed.) Summer wear was simply shorts, shirts and smocks. Girls wore flannel vests, skirts, knickers, combinations and jerseys in the winter, while on hot summer days they wore only light, specially made sun garments.

Good food was regarded as essential, especially for children who spent most of their life in the open air. It brought increased vitality and a more vigorous metabolism, and Wilkinson's report gave details of the quantities of food each child received in order to take in the required amounts of vitamins A B, C and D.

The food was rich in fats – almost a pound per boy each week, apart from what was present in the unskimmed milk fresh from the neighbouring farm. For boys the milk ration was a little more than half a pint a day, with girls drinking almost three-quarters of a pint. Vegetables, grown in the Heritage gardens, were cooked slowly to prevent vitamins being destroyed by heat, and potatoes were cooked in their jackets to retain vitamin B. Fresh farm eggs were available once a week and fresh fruit was usually available at least once a week. Only wholemeal bread was used: about a pound and a half per boy each day.

'Thus in quality and quantity,' this section concluded, 'the food leaves nothing to be desired. The boys, with very few exceptions, put on weight

From the 'Spectator', 1930: 'When you see these children being carried into the operating ward with a smile on their faces; and when you see them lying in all sorts of positions, some face-down, some flat on their backs, others slung by neck or ankles, but so brave, so patient, so keen to do anything that their twisted limbs can compass, you see the spirit that makes England great.

'Here is a little Welsh boy's card, which he wrote for me with his right foot as he lay in his cot. He was born without any arms. Now he dresses himself, using his chin as well as his feet, washes his teeth by holding a mug with one big toe and a toothbrush with the other, models in clay, reads and writes exceptionally well for a boy of his age, and looks a picture of health with his alert, grey-green eyes.'

Dennis Gobbee's memories, 1926: 'We were met at Cooksbridge Station by the ambulance, which was called the mustard pot because of its colour, and later when it was worn out we had a new one which was dark blue and this was aptly named the ink pot.

'My first night was spent in one of the Kitchener huts in a howling gale, and as it had a tin roof the noise of the rain was very frightening. The following morning we were woken by the loud ringing of a handbell, which summoned us to wash and get dressed, our outfit being short trousers in a dark shade of blue and a smock of the same colour. To complete the outfit we each had a cape to protect us against the weather.

'Breakfast was the next item, and this consisted of porridge and brown bread and margarine and a beaker of tea.'

DIET SHEET IN THE 1927 REPORT

Monday

Breakfast	Porridge; hot milk; bread and butter
Dinner	Lentil & vegetable soup; potatoes; suet & raisin puddings
Tea	Bread & butter with jam or treacle; tea

Tuesday

Breakfast	Coffee; bread & butter; fruit or porridge in winter
Dinner	Meat with cabbage, potatoes and bread; milk puddings
Tea	Bread & butter with treacle; tea

Wednesday

Breakfast	Hot milk, cocoa; bread & butter; apples in summer, marmalade in winter
Dinner	Meat pudding with cabbage and potatoes; bread; milk puddings
Tea	Bread & butter with jam; tea

Thursday

Breakfast	Hot milk; bread & butter; porridge in winter
Dinner	Irish stew, bread; suet pudding; fruit or dried fruit
Tea	Bread & butter; figs or dates; tea

Friday

Breakfast	Hot milk; tea; bread & butter; porridge in winter
Dinner	Vegetable soup; bread; potatoes; suet pudding with treacle
Tea	Bread & butter with jam; tea

Saturday

Breakfast	Coffee; apples in summer, marmalade in winter; bread & butter; hot milk
Dinner	Roast beef with cabbages and potatoes; bread; suet pudding with gravy
Tea	Bread & butter with treacle; tea

Sunday

Breakfast	Cocoa; bread & butter; eggs; apples; hot milk
Dinner	Cold meat with beetroot and potatoes; bread; milk or suet pudding with fruit or custard
Tea	Bread & butter with jam; tea

steadily. After the period spent at home for the holidays, the gain in weight for a few weeks is very rapid. The boys look extremely healthy and, in spite of the crippling effects of disease, the average boy tends to be robust.

'Animal spirits, though properly controlled, are very much in evidence; little of their occupation is sedentary and most of their work is done with their hands. Their physical existence, therefore, approaches closely the ideal, and this is very necessary in order to establish, in bodies already crippled, a constitution which will be proof against disease and debility.'

Not surprisingly, former pupils sometimes give a rather different account of what they were given to eat. Phyllis Garrett remembers the girls lining up outside the dining room and marching in to find their places. They had to salute the head girl, who was holding up the Union Jack.

'Breakfast consisted of porridge, brown bread, a knob of marge and black treacle. The plate was covered with black treacle. You didn't know what to do with your bread to spread it. A cup of tea, badly stewed. For lunch we had all sorts. One day we had suet pudding with black treacle on. Next day what was left over was served us as doughboys – it was vile.'

Doris Carter recalls that every bit of food had to be eaten.

'If you left it, you had to sit there until you changed your mind. A little boy called Jakey, who'd come to the Heritage with rickets, was very good at eating my food for me. But if you persisted in not eating it, they'd push it into your mouth.'

Phyllis Garrett (then Phyllis Gane) has a similar story.

'I can remember one morning I was sat at the table, and down comes my porridge. I went to put my spoon in to eat it, and it was one solid lump. When they cleared the tables I sent the porridge back. Down it came again, and they said I had to eat it. I was about 13 at the time, and no way was I going to eat it, so I sat there all day with the porridge in front of me. Twice it was warmed up, and still I wouldn't eat it. About eight o'clock that night matron came in and said "Are you going to eat that, Gane?", and I said "No." "Well,' she said, "I can't send you to bed hungry," and she brought me in a nurse's meal. It was delicious. I can remember it as though it was yesterday – cottage pie. When I went back to the dormitory all the girls thought I was very hungry, but I had the last laugh on them.

'Potatoes were always cooked in their skins: never peeled, never baked. Sundays I always hated. We used to have cold meat with salad, and it was nothing to find a slug in your lettuce leaf. The times I was caught coming out of the dining room with the lettuce leaf up my knickers ready for the Angora rabbits we kept!

'Once a week it was medicine night. That was liquorice – a brown powder mixed with water. It was absolutely vile. One night I didn't want to drink mine. I was by an open window, and I chucked it out on the concrete. We had a frost that night, and next morning there was my liquorice frozen for all to see. Needless to say, I had to have a double dose that night. Never again!'

'The porridge bowl, plate and beaker, all being of aluminium, soon got dented.

'When breakfast was finished the boy at the head of each table stood up and issued instructions to clear the tables "the Chailey way" – by numbers. Woe betide you if you dropped anything, because if you did you had to start all over again, and quite often the culprit was "bashed" in the hall afterwards by the boys at his table.'

'Matron was a very stern lady. She had very red hair, and she had a little cap on, with her bun sticking out the back. There was another lady who used to float after her – she was dressed in blue and had a white, flowing veil. I don't know exactly what she was doing.'

A photograph appearing in a programme for a Golden Apple event in 1931 with the caption 'Drumming in the success of the Matinee Appeal by a special "Roll" to welcome HRH the Duchess of York'. [Sport & General Press Agency]

Far From Home

For many years Chailey was chiefly a residential school, drawing children from all round the country. Some of them never got home: they had been discarded by their families. Most of the others went home briefly for holidays (although only after a formal letter had given 'permission' for this) and, because it was difficult for most people to travel, otherwise saw their parents only on fleeting visits to Chailey. These visits were not exactly encouraged.

Doris Carter was admitted to Chailey in 1935 at the age of five after a very bad case of measles, which affected her eyes and made her very weak. Her family lived close by, in Lewes, but she rarely saw them.

'It was once a month, and that was a calendar month – so sometimes nearly five weeks between visits. We didn't have chairs in our dormitory, but my mother and father would find some to sit on when they came. There was no cup of tea for them or anything like that.

'I was very homesick. A Clarke's bread van would come to the Heritage from Lewes, and I used to mark my day by that van. When I did eventually go home, at the age of seven, it took me a long time to adjust. Staying indoors was a problem, because I'd lived outside for two and a half years. I hadn't seen cars for ages, and it was very frightening on the high street. I was also terrified that I might have to go back.'

Jean Tweed, who had two spells at Chailey with dislocated hips, recalls a time when an outbreak of chickenpox led to a gap of three months between visits.

'That was very hard for a youngster,' she says. 'I remember finally going home just before I was ten, and my parents arranging a birthday party for me. It was strange, because I hardly knew the other children.'

Rules were rules in those days, and it took a pretty tough parent to resist them.

'I was transferred to Chailey from Bevendean isolation hospital in Brighton,' recalls Ann Agnew, 'and the authorities hadn't even told my parents. That was in 1947. Father insisted on being able to see me immediately, although they said he'd just missed visiting time and would have to wait for almost another month. They finally agreed on condition that my parents didn't make me cry. When my sister was born they brought her to the gate so they could wave.'

'When I remembered home, I missed [my sister] Gladys' company,' wrote Hilda Ashcroft (1923–26) 'for we had been very close and still are. She was only two when I left to go to Chailey, and I know she missed me, too. We were both happy to see each other again when I came home on holiday and always shared a bed.

'First thing every morning she would snuggle up close and ask "Where's old Floppy?", picking up my paralysed arm and nursing it like a baby. I read to her a lot and we went through the Beatrix Potter books so many times that Peter Rabbit, Jemima Puddleduck and Flopsy Bunny were like old friends.'

'For some reason my brother wasn't allowed to come and visit. Once, as a special treat, my mother smuggled him into the grounds, and we spoke through an open window.'

Dressing for home visits could be something of an ordeal, as Tony Williams recalls.

'You weren't allowed to wear your own clothes at the Heritage. They were put away, and you wore the uniform. If you'd last gone home during the summer, you'd find that by the time you put them on again for Christmas they were too small and out of fashion.'

Doreen Quibell joined the colony as a staff nurse in 1948.

'Visiting time was Sunday afternoon once a month,' she recalls. 'It was very difficult, as families didn't have much money. They came by train to Haywards Heath, and there was an hourly bus to the King's Head, the nearest stop to the Heritage. Then they had to walk, although occasionally a Chailey vehicle would meet the bus. A bus came up from Brighton after 1950. The grandfather of one of the patients was a bus driver, and he was allowed to work on Sunday and bring the bus to Chailey, stay for visiting time and take them back again.'

It was Doreen's future husband, Dr Quibell, who persuaded the Southdown bus company to rearrange their timetable so that that buses would arrive at the King's Head at time which would coordinate with trains and buses arriving from other directions.

'Imagine a grandma with rheumatic knees,' she adds, 'who leaves the Norfolk coast at 6am and goes to London, then down to Haywards Heath, then the hourly bus to the King's Head, then a walk all the way to the hospital side of the Heritage unless a lift happens along. A short visit; and then the journey in reverse. This particular grandmother visited a girl who, because of her handicap, wouldn't be accepted in the United States where her mother had moved with her American husband.

WENDY'S FAMILY

During the 1960s, at the instigation of the inspirational senior medical social worker Yenny Snider, the Heritage found 'substitute parents' for children who rarely or never saw their families. Angela Wigglesworth and her husband were among the first of them.

'We had three young children of our own, and I thought it would be enjoyable for us all to make contact with a child who didn't have a home to go to. I phoned Chailey and was invited to meet three-year-old Wendy. She was just three days older than my youngest child. I remember being quite nervous, but within a few moments of being in the ward her severe handicaps were forgotten and she was just a child.

'Over the years she would visit us at weekends, at Christmas and at Easter. I have happy memories of her when she was young, sitting on our kitchen table helping my daughter make cakes, and of the children pushing her wheelchair round our garden for Easter treasure hunts. In later years she liked to peel potatoes at the kitchen sink for Sunday lunch and tell me about her favourite pop stars.

'Wendy died in her mid-twenties. I always felt that I didn't do enough for her, but we did give her a family of her own to talk about with the other children at Chailey.'

'I remember with great admiration several grandmothers like that who found themselves guardians to their grandchildren. One of them was left to pick up the pieces when her daughter died and the father abandoned seven children who were now all in care – and not all together. She was a widow and a pensioner, and she lived in a council flat. She wrote to the older ones and visited each in turn. She came down to the Heritage from London on trains and buses. Her knees and her feet were bad. We gave her eggs and toast and tea, and she returned home in the afternoon, worn out.'

Janet McCausland, a probationer nurse in 1952, remembers a young girl from Wales called Barbara, who often waited a long time between visits.

'It was a long way from home, and once or twice I remember that she was longing to see her mum but the weather was bad so that she couldn't visit. She'd be months without seeing her, and I remember her being very distressed.'

Elaine Baldock first worked as a nurse in the early 1950s and remembers small kindnesses to girls such as Barbara.

'A lot of the children came from up north, which meant that their parents couldn't visit, and local parents (from Uckfield, say) would 'adopt' them, bringing extra sweets. A very happy day, that was. The bus only came as far as the King's Head then, and I used to walk to the Heritage from the bus stop at ten o'clock when I was on nights. I wouldn't do it now!'

By the 1960s the problem had found official recognition.

'If parents were unable to visit,' recalls Mary Sheppard, 'and there were many who didn't, an "official visitor" was found to take their place. I was one of the first nurses to become a "visitor" – and I befriended a little boy with no legs, and he is still my friend 33 years on.'

Lewes Motor Car Club's 'Cripples' Outing', July 1923. [Eric Jenner]

Daphne Hewitt recalls the isolation of Chailey:

'When you went home for the holidays the world was a very strange place. You'd hardly travelled on a bus or train. Many of us were insecure – very timid and unworldly.

'I hardly saw my parents. There was an epidemic of measles at one time, and no visitors were allowed. I never saw my sisters until I came home. When I was about 12 I was playing with a friend by one of the gates, and I looked up and saw a girl staring at me. I asked her if she was Margery. She asked if I was Daphne. I still feel that my three sisters are closer to each other than to me.'

A visit to Tidemills by the Bishop of London (above), and some exercises on the beach with the Newhaven cliffs as a backdrop (below). This was the open air life taken to its bracing limit.

A Life on the Ocean Wave

*I*n 1924 the Heritage opened a new facility by the sea which put its bracing fresh air philosophy into extreme practice. The marine hospital at Tidemills was the gift of the Warren family. A long line of ex-Admiralty huts was erected on the shingle near Bishopstone, where a small community of fishermen, pensioners and Southern Railway employees occupied a cluster of low buildings close to the remains of the former flour mill which gave the place its name – the tides which once powered the wheel would now sometimes flood the Heritage buildings. There was a railway halt and nothing else.

'I remember the first time I saw Tidemills,' wrote a former teacher in the first issue of Heritage magazine in 1948. 'It was an early spring day, and I had travelled there by train from London. The day was sunny, but with a distinct 'nip' in the air, and I was glad to be wearing a light overcoat. At Tidemills I found that the boys were wearing very few clothes and, so tough were they that they didn't seem to feel the cold. They glowed with an inward vitality which put me to shame.'

Photographs and films show the boys performing exercises on the shingle and playing in the water, the most disabled being lowered into the sea in large nets. The adults are wearing several layers of clothing, while the lads wear nothing but shorts.

'Later on,' continued the teacher, identified only as 'J.C.', 'I found that the Tidemills boys knew all the ways of keeping warm. They played on the lee side of the building out of the full force of the wind. They built themselves 'camps' in the shingle, which sheltered them. In fact they were knowledgeable, weather-wise young men.

'The centre of each ward was the main hospital corridor, and to teach in a ward was like teaching in "High Street, China". The peaceful atmosphere of the school room was noticeably lacking, and it was only necessary to start any lesson which required some degree of concentration on the part of the pupil for the whole 'street' to become alive with traffic of every sort. Usually, however, lessons were taught on the solarium. Beds were wheeled out there, and if it wasn't too hot or too cold or too windy the lesson could proceed.

'It was for its happy, informal atmosphere that I best remember Tidemills. When the tide and weather were right, boys, nurses and teachers went bathing, and boys who were unable to walk were able to swim. Whole evenings were spent in the boat, fishing for flounders and whiting; and I have known the time when enough fish were caught to supply everyone with breakfast the next morning.

'It is a polite fiction that the fish which we gave to the Bishop of London every year were caught by the young fishermen of Tidemills. They provided an admirable opportunity for the bishop to say every year that all the cats followed his car when he returned from Tidemills to the palace. Strangely enough, the story never failed to draw the laughter of us all. Perhaps, leading the simple life that we did, we were able to laugh at simple jokes.'

A less than rigorous account from the Coming of Age book: 'Historically the spot is full of interest. Alfred the Great had a castle not far off. Tradition has it that on the very spot upon which Tidemills is built the Danes landed, to plunder and maraud Sussex.

'In later days Louise Philippe landed here, to visit Mr William Catt, and discuss with him the possibility of harnessing the tides, for scientific and practical purposes. Remains of the mills are still to be seen, hence the name – Tidemills. Descendants of Mr Catt still come to Tidemills to discuss nowadays how best to help the Heritage.'

From the 1948 book (by which time Tidemills had closed):

'Here can be seen a shipbuilding class in progress, for whether at work or at play, as much time as possible is spent in the open air.,
In the distance is the lighthouse at Newhaven, and the arrival and departures of the cross-channel steamers never failed to interest the boys.

'Tidemills is, in itself, another type of lighthouse, guiding the crippled boys into the desired harbour of healthy independence. After operations at Chailey the boys are transferred to Tidemills to convalesce, and during the Christmas and summer holidays, when the Chailey schoolboys go home, those who are bedridden, or not considered fit to travel by the doctors, go to Tidemills and greatly benefit by the change of air and scene.'

Most of the Tidemills boys (there were no facilities for girls) were suffering from infantile or spastic paralysis. The criteria for sending them to what was known as Chailey's 'marine annexe' were explained in a report written by the resident medical officer:

'A consideration of educational as opposed to remedial requirements determines to which department boy is sent. If his chief need is to learn a trade and he does not require hospital treatment, he is sent to the Kitchener Heritage. A boy who requires treatment in hospital is admitted there, so that when he has finished hospital treatment his education may be uninterrupted. A boy who requires more treatment than is compatible with life at the Kitchener Heritage and yet who does not require hospital treatment is sent to Tidemills.

'Tidemills is used for boys who require intensive physical treatment over a long period: more time during the day can be given to treatment than at the Boys' Heritage. At the same time a schoolmaster continues their education. This is not of an advanced nature: the younger children require more constant surgical supervision, and it is they also who benefit most from the additional treatment obtainable, and therefore it is the younger ones who are usually sent.'

A 400ft corridor ran from room to room the entire length of the building, while there were verandahs to the seaward side. Water lapped under the floor beneath the beds. One of the Tidemills nurses later recalled 'struggling to force the shutters to keep out the harvest tide with a force eight gale blowing'. Hours were long, work was hard, and all the old iron beds had to be pulled out on to the solarium each morning and brought in again at night, 'unless the weather dictated a more frequent repetition'.

Dennis Gobbee came to Chailey from Bedford in 1926 and was moved to Tidemills two years later. He had, he wrote in *Heritage News*, never seen the sea before, and it struck him as very rough.

'One of my many memories of Tidemills were the very heavy gales we used to get, and also very bad sea fogs. On several occasions cargo ships would run aground on the beach, which for us boys as an exciting event. Another thing we particularly liked was when the mail boats left Newhaven Harbour. In those days they were on time. One used to leave at precisely 12 noon and the one coming from Dieppe would enter the harbour at 4pm (whatever the weather). All the ships belonged to the Southern Railway, and some of their names were the Brighton, Paris, Worthing and Rouen.

'Another regular event was on Tuesdays when a large cargo boat would anchor outside the harbour. This was a coal boat, and we boys called it "Blacky".

'As there was considerable wind from the sea, we were able to fly kites. These we made with bamboo cane and brown paper. One problem was the string needed to fly them, and this was usually overcome by asking the nurses for thread for sewing purposes. Of course this was used for flying our kites.

'At Easter time the boys were given tops and marbles, which we believed were donated by a well-wisher.

'As the hospital and classrooms were built on the beach we used to build camps by shovelling the shingle into the shape of a ship (some of them quite big). We would collect all the old driftwood washed up from the sea and build cabins inside at the back end of the ship, and then cover with shingle except for the doorway. The mast would be made of a large piece of wood, lashed down with strong string and ropes and decorated with flags and bunting. A competition was held to see whose camp was the best.

'There was always something to do and see at Tidemills. Fishing boats, the shrimpers, old wrecks washed upon the beach. We swam in the sea and there was cricket and football.'

This maritime idyll was to be brought to an end by the second world war, when fears of an invasion led to the clearance of the beaches. Chailey was paid compensation, but the Tidemills buildings were used for target practice, which meant that the settlement, Heritage huts and all, was never lived in again. Only the foundations survive today as a reminder of this Heritage-by-the-sea.

'To raise funds we used to collect flat pebbles from the beach, make some white paint with chalk and water, let them dry and the boys who could paint good pictures did their part. They were varnished and sold to people who came along the beach. They made good paperweights.'

The white cliffs of Seaford Head can be seen in the distance as the boys frolic in the waves.

Above: Some of the girls with the Bishop of London outside St Helen's Chapel.

Below: The Princess Elizabeth Clinic for tiny Babes at Chailey Clump.

Girls Heritage, Chailey Clump.—
The Princess Elizabeth Clinic for Tiny Babes.

43

Heritage Heyday

*C*hanges have been continuous at Chailey over the century – new ideas, new buildings, new developments far too numerous to detail in a readable account – but the late–1920s to mid–1930s was arguably the finest period of Grace Kimmins' imperious rule at the Heritage.

At the girls' site (the New Heritage) the Princess Elizabeth Clinic for Tiny Babes (PEC) was founded by Seymour Obermer, with backing from the *Daily Mirror*'s Pip, Squeak and Wilfred: their pets' house, Mirror Grange, travelled through Britain and abroad, raising funds for the project. All the children here were under one year old.

'Visitors always linger,' wrote Mrs Kimmins. 'Facing the building is the happy playground of the babes and toddlers. The children live, eat and sleep in the open air all the year round, and visitors always exclaim when they see them under these conditions even during the severe winter months, but the results prove without doubt that this type of life is the best possible for the children. Many of them are in an almost hopeless state when they arrive, but respond very quickly to the expert care and attention which they receive.'

The girls' chapel was built in 1931, the year in which Pax Est, the headquarters of the Prince Louise Own Heritage Girl Guides was opened. The two-storey Jubilee block followed in 1936, on a 'slum clearance' site: the hutments used by soldiers during the war 'were not new when sent down from the War Office,' Grace Kimmins reported, 'and, having been moved from place to place as occasion required, are now incapable of further movement, and are leaking and rat-infested.'

The new block was, of course, designed to take full advantage of sun and air, and an uncovered first-floor balcony looked south to the chapel and the Bernhard Baron schoolroom with the trees of Chailey Clump beyond.

'It well may be that in the near future this type of building (so fully approved by educationalists and the medical world alike) may be widely adopted elsewhere, comprising as it does both dignity, usefulness and, above all, providing the happiest environment for the bedridden children.

'From this balcony they can watch the life of the girls' colony as, like a human tide, it flows by them to church and school and play. They form the most enthusiastic of audiences for a stoolball match, Margaret Morris dancing and outdoor singing classes. It is so right that such a building should contain so much variety, but, alas, not all buildings can have such a lovely setting.'

By today's standards, of course, the Heritage was a regimented institution, with a sometimes harsh enforcement of the rules. Doris Carter remembers having her tonsils out at the age of five, and of her mother's horror upon arriving for a special visit to discover her comatose daughter having boiled egg forced down her throat.

'It was meal time and the meal was egg,' she says simply. 'There was blood on my egg, because I'd only just come round from the anaesthetic, and my mother went absolutely mad and made them stop. She almost hit

Hilda Ashcroft remembers:

'A few years after my arrival at Chailey, the Princess Elizabeth Clinic was built behind the school. This was for real babies, some as young as six weeks, so tiny and wasted tht they looked like skinned rabbits.

'Those with twisted bones and crooked spines were confined to bed face down, kept in place with soft webbing straps that I was taught to make on a sewing machine.

'When the clinic sister was away our school sister was in charge, and I helped to feed and nurse the babies after their bath. It was wonderful to hold and cuddle them close, and I loved them all dearly. I still like holding babies, perhaps especially so because I never had any of my own.'

the nurse. But that's the way things were, then: rules were rules. On one occasion I was put on a potty on my bed and I toppled over, wetting it. I was shut in an airing cupboard for the night.

'I can't abide boiled egg to this day, and I suffer from claustrophobia – and I'm sure both can be attributed to what happened to me then.'

Barbara Booth (née Goudie) caught polio just before her fourth birthday, and she was at the Heritage from 1935–36. Her stock of memories is vivid, and includes a few uncomfortable ones: 'Trying to keep brown woollen stockings up with only the elastic in my knicker legs. Always wanting to go to the toilet when in church, and always wondering how the staff saw me wriggling (as children do in these circumstances) from their boxes at the back. Standing in the frost queueing for breakfast, and putting my hands inside my gym slip to keep warm. This was not ladylike, and my punishment was to scrub the floor of the hut: why this for a six-year-old who was unable to kneel, perhaps someone can tell me. Again, on a cold morning, getting dressed in bed, being picked up and put in the middle of the room and having to dress on the floor (again with the same punishment).'

And a poignant question: 'Why I was not allowed to play with the lovely doll Queen Mary gave me I do not know. It was put on a shelf, and there it stayed.'

MIRROR GRANGE

Mirror Grange was an 8ft x 7ft model, with furniture to a 1:12 scale, designed by Maxwell Ayrton – joint architect of the Wembley Exhibition. It took nearly a year to build and was finished in December 1929.

Special tools had to be made, many of them from knitting needles tempered and shaped down to meet special cases. Tiny-gauge chisels were made to carve the thatch of the roof.

In the drawing room an income tax envelope lay on a used blotting pad on the bureau, while a 28-page reproduction of the Daily Mirror lay on a table. Each page was photographed so that every letter was clear: it was then printed on the thinnest photographic paper, the paper rubbed even thinner with pumice before the pages were pasted back to back and folded to represent a normal copy of the newspaper.

Mirror Grange was housed in the Princess Elizabeth Clinic (PEC).

'A fascinating assignment, but a nerve-wracking one,' wrote Kath Crittenden later, 'was to clean it out – with a dry paint brush.'

An aerial view of the boys' residential block on the common, St George's. The smock mill is said to stand at the very centre of Sussex. [Brenda Izzard]

But there were more pleasant interludes, too: 'We were allowed a small piece of the garden to cultivate. My mother sent me some marigold seeds to sow: this was probably the start of my love of gardening. On parents' day my mother would go home with a lovely bunch of primroses which I had picked in the woods.

'I remember sitting around a big table outside the kitchen and cutting up large blocks of salt. To make it more interesting we used to carve out houses before cutting it smaller. Many people have thought that the regime at Chailey was hard in those days. It may have been, but it wasn't cruel. It taught you to be independent and to carry through all tasks to the best of your ability.'

At Chailey's original site, the Old Heritage, change was incremental rather than dramatic (in 1937, for instance, Mrs Harcourt Rose presented the chapel with an east window, golden reredos and altar frontal as a coronation gift), but on the common the old Kitchener huts built by the boys during the first world war as their own accommodation were in 1932 replaced by the most ambitious building project of them all: the two-storey St George's. It was built of brick, all the external woodwork was of naturally weathered oak and the ventilating tower of the impressive dining hall, with its stone mullioned windows and minstrels' gallery, was covered with oak shingles. There were six dormitories, one of them named after the Warren family, who had given the land on which the building stood.

'The dining hall really looked a picture when the tables were set for meals,' wrote Kath Crittenden years later. 'Dark, highly polished Sussex oak tables and forms (benches), enhanced by the willow pattern crockery we used for meals. Brightly polished cutlery, cleaned every week, a scrubbed parquet floor and large open coal-burning fireplace finished the picture – really lovely, and never to be forgotten.'

Former teacher H.W. Leggatt: 'Every morning at exactly 9.30 all the masters, including the head, paraded in front of [Mrs Kimmins] in the council chamber, to be given our orders for the day, and to be told of anything special happening during the day, or of something you did wrong the previous day.

'When I came to the Heritage she had a dog called Bowser. For some uncanny reason he always knew where she was going. He was always about three minutes ahead of her, for which we and the children were very glad, for it enabled us to make sure that all was right – all windows open, all doors WIDE open. If they weren't she would at once open everything. She always threw any mats outside, and if any dirt came out she would at once send for the cleaner to know why they were dirty.'

As we have seen, substantial sums of money had been raised for St George's through the Golden Apple appeal and an apple tree design was therefore affixed above the main entrance. Schools across the world had been invited to contribute to the fund-raising, the contributions ranging from just under £60 (Eton College) to tuppence (Barcombe School, a few miles away from the Heritage). The Prince of Wales, later Edward VIII, had also dipped into his pocket (*see page 21*).

There were many other individual contributions from home and abroad, and the appeal was also supported by a radio broadcast (raising £918), legacies (£13,850), an article in the *Times* (£5,898) and a special matinee at the Regal Cinema, Seaford (£760). The Chailey children played their part, too, making items such as bookmarks and 'The Heritage Well Gummed Luggage Labels'. In all, the huge sum of £38,000 was raised.

The following year the old white smock mill next to St George's – wrecked in a great gale in January 1928 – was restored by public subscription. True, it was owned by the local council, but for the author John Galsworthy, who lived in West Sussex, the mill and its attendant yew were silent guardians of the Heritage colony:

'Away past the house, perhaps six hundred yards, stood a ghostly windmill, with a face like that of a dark-eyed white owl, made by the crossing of its narrow sails. With a black companion – a yew tree, cut to a pyramid form, on the central point in Sussex – it was watching us, for though one must presume it built of old time by man, it had taken charge up there against the sky with its owl's face and its cross, a Christo-Pagan presence.

'What exactly Paganism was we do not, and never shall, know; what exactly Christianism is, we are as little likely to discover; but here and there the two principles seem to have married and dwell together in amity. For Paganism believed in a healthy and joyful body; and Christianism in a soul superior thereto. And, where we were sitting that summer day, was the home of bodies wrecked yet learning to be joyful, and of souls not above the process.'

Crowds gather to celebrate the restoration of the windmill.
[Central News Ltd]

The Heritage's first patron, Princess Alice, Countess of Athlone, cuts a cake during her visit to mark the restoration of the windmill. [Alfieri Picture Service]

Tony Medhurst came to Chailey in 1935 suffering from infantile paralysis, and he was in the hospital until 1939.

'I was the youngest there for a time. I remember the food being served on aluminium plates and bowls, and that we had porridge for breakfast during the week and bread and milk on Sundays.

'Corporal Hayes was the orderly responsible for cleaning the ward. He used to spread tea leaves on the ward floor before sweeping it every morning. About once a week he polished the floor with Ronuk, using a bumper or donkey. It was also his job to get the boys prepared for operations and X-rays. He had been a soldier in the first world war. Corporal Hayes also accompanied the boys who were able to walk to the bathroom. It was obvious when operations were taking place because of the smell of ether.

'During the summer months – which always seemed hot in the thirties – we would lie on our beds covered only with a loin cloth. The beds had space for a shade to be fitted to keep the sun from eyes and heads. If anyone did start to burn, the staff would apply calamine lotion. In the winter months some boys would have UVR treatment, which was on a time basis, with loin cloths and rubber glasses being worn.

'I had to wear boots, calipers and a spinal jacket in bed. My boots were put in a bag to prevent the sheets being marked. I had electric treatment

Former teacher Leonard Holgate: 'The end of my three-month trial was getting near, and I didn't think I had much chance of coming back after the summer holidays. A few days before the end of term I was requested to go to matron's office, where Dame Grace, matron and the headmaster were waiting.

In her forthright manner, Dame Grace said: "Well, Mr Holgate, I don't think you will ever suit Chailey. Matron says you are obstinate, sister says you are rude, but the headmaster says the boys like you, and you could make a good teacher, and Dr Kimmins says you are a good cricketer. So I suppose you had better stay".'

Mr Holgate stayed for all of 42 years.

most days. When I started learning to walk again I had to try to keep my feet straight in line with the floorboards. I managed when I was about 7½ years of age. The boys with a TB problem had to sleep out on the balcony night and day, rain or shine.

'The ward gramophone was the same model as in the HMV advert, with a horn on the top of the set. The weeping willow near the corner of the balcony had a flat top, and was a very convenient area for us to throw some of the revolting fatty mutton sometimes served.'

In 1939 Mrs Kimmins pulled off another coup. An exhibition of royal and historic treasures, including Elizabeth I's dainty grey slippers and Charles I's ruffed and embroidered lawn and lace nightshirt, was held at 145 Piccadilly, formerly the home of the King and Queen. There were some 1300 exhibits, and visitors were asked to put money in a white windmill.

In November of that year the *Sussex Weekly News* reported that Princess Alice had attended a thanksgiving service in the chapel, and had been expected to bring a cheque for around £6,000 – a cheque that would be placed in a 'golden' casket made by one of the boys and florally decorated.

'Judge of the surprise to Mrs Kimmins, the tireless commandant and founder of the Heritage, and members of the governing body, when they found that the cheque was for, not £6,000, but £10,217. 10s 5d. Viscount Nuffield had given £4,000.'

In 1937 (rather later than one might have expected of her) Mrs Kimmins instigated a house system at Chailey, just like a traditional public school. Each of the three houses was named after a benefactor – Lord Llangattock (blue), Bernhard Baron (yellow) and Seymour Obermer (green) – and each had its captain, button badges and coloured bands for games.

'It was very well received by us all,' remembered Kath Crittenden later. 'We were very competitive and took pride in our various house activities. Each month matron would read the mark sheets, and either praised or reprimanded accordingly, and at the end of each summer term a shield was presented to the best house.'

But the storm clouds had already broken: war had been declared. The exhibition was forced to close much earlier than planned, the Heritage receiving a donation in compensation. In 1938 Mr J.C. Ionides had given the boys a playing field and cricket pavilion on land previously used for growing vegetables, but now the field swiftly reverted to a vegetable plot. The Heritage children practised their gas mask drill and had to recite their identity numbers every morning.

There were 'rumours of war' inside the colony, too.

Another War

At the outbreak of war Grace Kimmins was approaching 70 and might have been expected to offer a less robust response to the conflict than she had shown a quarter of a century before. Not so, however..

'Once again,' she was to write later, 'the word "impossible" was not to be found in the Heritage dictionary.'

At a time when new building work was generally at a standstill, she went fund-raising in order to enlarge the Princess Elizabeth Clinic and to provide a home for 'Blitzed Babies and Toddlers'. These were children who had been pulled out of bombed homes and air-raid shelters, and who were suffering from bronchitis and pneumonia or from the effects of stress.

The Queen, as patron of the Heritage, declared that 'the little sufferers would get exactly the right treatment and environment at Chailey.' Money was raised, largely by the British War Relief Society in America, and a site was found adjoining the Girls' Heritage.

The new building was opened in 1942. Each single-storey ward had a south-facing verandah and solarium, and a north terrace for maximum shade. The emphasis, as usual, was on fresh air 'which is the life-lung for the treatment of the two-to-five year old child for whom this home was provided'.

There were also a playroom, a kitchen, a paddling pool and a bathroom with tiny baths, gaily painted walls and floating ducks – a gift of the Heritage staff, past and present. An adjoining two-storey nurses' wing of 28 rooms and sitting room was the gift of the Bernhard Baron Trust.

The Duchess of Gloucester officially opened the home, bringing a message from the Queen with her. As the *Southern*

'Get on with the job,' the toddlers urged the builders of the home for blitzed babies, 'because the Queen is coming!'

Taking lunch in a sandbagged air raid shelter at the Girls' Heritage. [*Daily Mirror*]

Weekly News reported, the Stars and Stripes was flown alongside the Union Jack as a tribute to the large American contribution.

'Blitzed twins Malcolm and Donald Cameron were brought forward by a nurse to present to the Duchess a bouquet, and a blitzed babe in the arms of an American nursing sister had for her a soft toy made by a bedridden child for Prince William of Gloucester.

'Other gifts followed from boys and girls, including a large bouquet, a hand-wrought wooden bowl filled with apples and autumn leaves, a paper-knife made from the wood of the old windmill, a pair of carved wooden bellows, a cigarette box made of Sussex wood (for the Duke), a hot water bottle in embroidered cover, a cake made by the girls, an embroidered tablecloth and (for Prince William) a little woollen coat.'

Clearly Grace Kimmins hadn't lost her touch. Indeed, she seems to have been just a little too enthusiastic. In March 1943 she reported that the Heritage had admitted 71 blitzed babies, and that she had been advised to reduce the number to the agreed figure of 50.

Large sums were raised for Chailey in America during the early years of the war. Here Mrs Clark Minor, a delegate from the British War Relief Society Incorporated of the United States of America, is greeted by Uncle Sam and John Bull. [Keystone Press Agency]

A happy band of toddlers, playing during a visit by the Lord Mayor of London. [*Keystone Press Agency*/ Brenda Izzard]

'The toddlers have their own band,' she reported in the 1948 book, 'and really they play with a surprising amount of rhythm, and their teacher is a past mistress in not only gaining their affection, but in her careful training of these small children.

'It is only during the past few years that the great possibilities have been grasped of dealing effectively with the early stages of development, which are even more promising than at any later period. Psychologists and the more practical of the educational experts now, at long last, fully realise that the two-to-five years stage is far and away the most significant and precious of the child's life.'

The Chailey girls were doing their bit for the war effort, using their spare time knitting for the armed forces: 'three months for the Air Force, three for the Army, then the Navy', Phoebe Cockram recalled later.

The stringencies brought about by a debilitating war can no doubt be blamed for much of it, but there is no doubt that, after the glories of earlier years, the Heritage was at a low ebb. The blitzed baby home apart, the drift was steadily downwards.

'I remember when we were told about the hunt for the German battleship Bismarck, and the cheer that went up when we were told that it had been sunk. This was one morning when we were at breakfast.'

'A couple of
fellows left their
food, and they
were rationed all
weekend to half
an ounce of butter
and a spoonful
of jam.'

Food was necessarily poorer at a time of rationing. The catering manager had each child's ration book, and a typical weekday breakfast at St George's (where meals were eaten in silence) was described as 'porridge with salt (cheaper than sugar) and cold milk, followed by a slice of brown bread, a small square of margarine and marmalade, accompanied by a pint mug of tea'. Sunday breakfast was 'something special, no porridge, just brown bread and beef dripping . . . accompanied by a pint of cocoa. The bread was stale, usually three or four days old, and sliced into thick "doorsteps". There was great excitement one Easter Sunday when the only boiled egg of the year was served up.'

Lunch consisted of red meat ('sometimes whale meat'), either sliced or minced, plain boiled vegetables and potatoes boiled in their skins: 'an aluminium bowl was placed on the table for the skins, which we took off the potatoes as we ate them.' Puddings included apple and chocolate sponges and bread pudding, with semolina and tapioca as occasional alternatives.

A photograph of staff working at the various Heritage sites taken by the windmill around 1940.
[Hamlin's Photo-News Service/Brenda Izzard]

'Tea was a simple affair of brown bread with margarine, jam and a pint of tea. Special teas of sandwiches, cakes and jellies were for great occasions 'when Chailey was visited by members of the royal family and bishops'.

Margaret Davis, a patient from 1936 to 1939 with bovine TB, was once invited to tea with the Dame and a group of other children.

'She was a formidable character to a child of six, with her deep purple gown and starched hat, but what I remember most was the sandwiches. They were white like snow. I can't tell you what was in them, but I'd become accustomed to the TB diet of brown bread, and I just couldn't take my eyes off them.'

David Arnold, at Chailey for operations on his displaced hips from 1945–46, remembers the food as being 'terrible', with burnt mince a speciality. Occasionally, he says, there were dried bananas.

'They were flat and black, and like toffee to chew. Unforgettable!'

'The best bet was to be in hospital,' says Peter Winstanley (a pupil from 1944–47). 'That was luxury, and the food was like the Savoy. But in the school they had a cook from the army, and he made some concoction which he called cauliflower cheese. Nobody would eat it. To this day my wife will never put cauliflower cheese on my plate – it makes me physically sick.

'Education, like food, was better in the hospital. A man came from Hurstpierpoint College at one time to teach us algebra and so on. He'd take time with us. And the nurses were human – the only human side in Chailey was the hospital.

'Education was poor in the school. Fortunately I could read and write. The teachers were retired people, because this was wartime, and you were knocked down very quickly if you were deemed to be too clever. A friend of mine was called 'big head' by staff because he knew the answers.

'They were hard times, but of course there were some really tough boys in there, so perhaps they had to be like that. You learnt toughness.'

Children would sometimes die while at the Heritage, and Jean Tweed remembers a lack of mourning on the wards.

'Of course some of us would talk about it a bit among ourselves, but there was an attitude of "Let's get on with it" on the part of the staff. You weren't affected by it as far as they were concerned.'

Ron Mitchell, at the Heritage with polio during the 1940s, remembers this as a bleak time. A strict regime may have been necessary, he concedes, but it was, 'a weary place' and very cold.

'We had to keep the dormitories clean ourselves,' he recalls. 'We had a long stick with a block on the end, covered with material, and you had to swing this about the floor to polish it. I was wearing a caliper, and some had crutches and wheelchairs, but as long as you were able to do it you had to do the cleaning.

'If you were naughty they made you sleep in the corridor with just a blanket on you. That doesn't sound very awful, but it was very bleak. If you didn't like the food your only hope was to wrap it in a handkerchief and smuggle it out: otherwise you'd have to eat it. You weren't allowed to wear your own clothes, and they never cut my hair, so it grew very long. You

The children found ways to supplement their diet. There were blackberries, hazelnuts and wild strawberries on the common, while chestnuts from the Heritage trees and potatoes dug in the nearby fields were cooked in the hot ashes of the boilers.

Sweets and chocolates would sometimes be provided by American and Canadian troops camped on the common and, inevitably, there was 'the thrill of scrumping apples and pears, which we did from all over the orchards and gardens'.

'We would parade outside for breakfast during the spring and summer mornings at 7.30 and would watch the planes coming back from missions.'

Locally based soldiers were a hit with the Heritage boys.

'When the Allies were preparing to invade, they would have mock battles all around us on Chailey Common North. It was great for us boys – tanks, thunderflashes etc. Some of us had our first fags from the Canadians. I remember Sweet Caprol and British Consuls.'

were supposed to stand on your own two feet, but I don't think a bit of sympathy would have gone amiss. A couple of the boys tried to do a runner, and they were caught outside the Heritage. I remember that the police were involved, and they were punished for that.

'One good thing I remember is that there were soldiers close by, and they'd sometimes come into the grounds and play games with us. They wore blue jackets and red ties – I think they were from a military hospital.'

David Arnold recalls Canadian soldiers taking the children round the gardens of Sheffield Park (somewhat overgrown during the war), as well as visits from entertainers such as Vera Lynn, Johnny Morris and 'Uncle Mac'. Those on the wards had regular visits from the imposing Mrs Kimmins.

'She was very old fashioned, always dressed in a purple matron's uniform, and I think people were a bit frightened of her. She'd look round to see what needed doing, even peering into the corners to make sure the place was clean. But she spoke nicely to us boys, and she'd ask us if we had any complaints.'

In 1944, an HMI visit revealed, the boys' school had no certificated teacher other than the headmaster, a situation which it was agreed should be remedied once the war was over. The report criticised the practice of teaching girls in two groups only, the age range (from six to 16 years) being far too great to be efficient. One teacher was responsible for no fewer than 70 children in the nursery school, and the girls' school as a whole needed 'a competent and experienced headmistress'.

Finding good nursing staff was difficult, too. The additional commitments the Heritage had taken on in the war years meant that its staff had received less leisure, off-duty time or holidays than nurses employed elsewhere. In 1943, and again the following year, Chailey sought to join a scheme for orthopaedic training which would enable it to award the certificate to its nurses, but to do so it needed to appoint a Sister Tutor 'and the necessary staff.

Not only was this impossible, but in 1945 the girls' matron claimed that she had been obliged to reduce the number of children by thirty, and that a further reduction was inevitable because eight students on a training scheme at Chailey were due to return to London. The matron gave the total number of vacancies as 36, of which 24 were nursing posts. The Queen Elizabeth block was closed at Christmas that year because of staff shortages, the children and their nurses being absorbed into other wards.

The problem grew worse, and in the summer of 1947 St George's had to be closed so that nurses could take a holiday. A further reduction in the number of children was forecast if staffing levels failed to rise. Advertising in local and Irish newspapers was tried, but it was recognised that without being able to offer training leading to the orthopaedic certificate the Heritage would be unable to attract either trained staff or student nurses.

Keeping the place warm was yet another problem. The Ministry of Fuel and Power cannily cited the colony's open-air medical treatment as a reason for cutting its fuel consumption by all of 35 per cent. In July 1947 the deputy medical director warned that unless the fuel position improved during the coming winter, the governors would have to consider closing a large part of the Heritage.

'The temperature in the wards last winter was a constant source of anxiety,' he wrote, 'and we must consider carefully whether we are justified in exposing children with active tuberculosis and other diseases to the risks involved in nursing them in such conditions again.'

The following winter was one of the coldest on record, and in the February Murray Levick told the Ministry that 'our allocation has previously been barely enough to get us through a normal winter, but

'The windmill at St George's used to be our tuck shop, where we could buy sweets for a penny, given to us by our house master Mr White, who was a Spitfire pilot earlier in the war. He married the matron.'

When the Germans started the bombing raids, the boys in the upstairs dormitories slept in passages on mattresses which had to be picked up every morning before we could get into breakfast, and then put down again after tea. Boys in the downstairs dormitories slept under their beds on an extra mattress.'

Canadian soldiers camped on the common would often visit the Heritage and were firm favourites with the children. Here they prepare Christmas gifts, one of them properly attired for the occasion. [Canadian Military photograph]

owing to the fact that the last eight weeks have been exceptionally severe, much more fuel has been burnt'. He reminded them that the hospitals and schools comprised separate departments and were not heated by one central boiler.

Although fuel supplies were eventually restored to reasonable levels, conditions in the open wards continued to pose problems for the nursing staff: the matron even suggested that nurses in the Princess Elizabeth Clinic should be supplied with a warmer out-fit, and that 'this should take the form of a skiing costume with felt boots'. Other suggestions included 'Burberry-type clothing', ex-Government surplus stock and overshoes which might give better support than fleece-lined boots.

The children's clothing was reviewed at the same time. Every boy was to have a tweed jacket, while the old red jerseys were to be replaced by collarless ones 'of fawn foundation flecked with various colours'. The number of light blue shirts (eccentrically worn over the jerseys, as they were 'more easily washed') was doubled

As in the first world war, although on a smaller scale, Mrs Kimmins offered facilities at the Heritage for recuperating soldiers. [Hamlin of Brighton]

to six per boy, with lightweight aertex shirts worn in summer. The older boys wore long, dark brown corduroy trousers, switching to khaki drill shorts in warmer weather. The rest of the wardrobe consisted of a towelled dressing gown, mitten gloves, sandals for indoor use, proofed gaberdine capes and interlock underpants 'instead of unbleached calico'. Protective overalls for craftwork were issued, too.

The girls' winter clothing comprised red cloaks, red pullovers, pinafore frocks and blouses, and – in the summer months – divided skirts and aertex blouses. Changes were made to both sets of seasonal wear. Each girl was to have a dressing gown, one cotton frock, one moygashel skirt, a grey flannel skirt or pinafore frock, three blouses and woollen stockings. Grey cardigans replaced red pullovers and blue ribbons the red braid, while bedsocks were generally available to all patients at the girls' heritage.

Meanwhile the colony's financial situation had grown steadily worse. In 1941–43 receipts were £70,500 against payments of £38,908, providing a generous surplus of £31,691. By 1944–45, however, receipts were down to little more than £45,000 and barely covered outgoings. During the following two years deficits were recorded, of £9,597 and £6,476 respectively.

A report presented by the deputy medical director in May 1948 revealed how badly standards had fallen. The administration during the first year of the war, when Levick was recalled to active service and the governing body thus lost its chairman, was described as 'inadequate and faulty'. The matron, with a staff of only six trained nurses, was responsible for the care and protection of 280 staff and children. Greatly overworked, 'spending night after night for years patrolling all departments of the colony, frequently during air raids', she had been refused secretarial help and had even, in June 1943, been told to reduce her staff.

The headmaster had experienced problems, too. Although discipline had improved since his appointment in 1942, when the boys had been 'out of hand', there was, he complained, a persistent interference with the school timetable. 'Far too much time' was spent in rehearsals in chapel: one boy had kept a diary showing that he had lost 96 school hours in one term in this way.

There were other complaints of a kind which would have been unthinkable only a few years earlier: the unannounced arrival of visitors on the wards, the lack of full receipts for money collected by the matron and headmaster, the ignoring of requests for repairs and urgent replacements and – the ultimate – 'a very serious difference of opinion between the founder and certain members of the governing body and the staff which might result in several resignations and do serious damage to the Heritage'.

The Medical Council, concerned at 'the widespread dissatisfaction and misunderstanding', now decided that 'only immediate remedial action can avert a crisis which may reach serious dimensions'. Several recommendations were made. Matrons should be allowed to run their departments without interference. Official and unofficial visitors should be received by the matrons, as much advance notice as possible having been given: the Medical Council was particularly concerned that Ministry of Health

'Bomber' Hudson: 'I travelled by train through wartime England, and arrived at the Heritage carrying my gas mask in September 1942, aged six years.

'My introduction to life at Chailey was to be ushered into the great dining hall at St George's with 120 other weepy-eyed boys. We stood behind the forms at three tables running the full length of the dining hall. On a plate in front of each boy was a sausage and a piece of thick brown bread (no margarine, as there was a war on).

'The house-master, Mr White known as Whitey, called for silence and grace. I closed my eyes: "For what we are about to receive may the Lord make us truly thankful. Amen."

'I opened my eyes and my sausage was gone. Lesson number one for life thereafter was, never close your eyes for anything.'

officials had arrived for their most recent inspection before the matron was informed that it was taking place.

The Medical Council said the case for a hospital secretary conversant with hospital administration, and who would also act as secretary to the governing body, had been clearly demonstrated and should be appointed as soon as possible – someone, it added somewhat acidly, who should be 'a properly qualified hospital officer and not one who, whatever his social graces and other experience, has no proper training in hospital administration.'

The residential accommodation provided for the girls was condemned by the Medical Council and it was decided that, with the exception of those under treatment, they should be sent home to attend normal school until proper accommodation was available. And the Council re-stated its long-standing request that accounts should be drawn up showing the cost to the Heritage of each child in a hospital bed, the governors being asked to 'find some way to make these figures available'.

The professionals had arrived, and they were knocking at the door. In 1946 Mrs Kimmins had written to the governors asking to be relieved from her responsibilities as chief administrator.

'It has been brought to my notice from various sources,' her letter began, 'that there is dissatisfaction amongst certain members of the governing body and staff regarding the administration of the Heritage.

'Since Miss Rennie and I first founded Chailey 43 years ago, and particularly since she died, though her indelible influence on the place will live for ever, I have been its chief administrator and I hope I have reason to be proud of the work. At the same time I hope I shall always be the first to face facts, and there can be no doubt that advancing years and certain physical disabilities now make it impossible for me to continue with the day by day adminstration.'

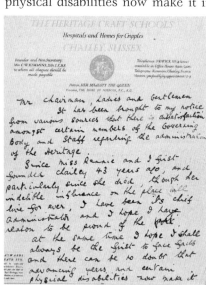

Mrs Kimmins' letter, asking to be relieved of her role as the Heritage's chief administrator.

She did not, she made clear, intend to stop working. Far from diminishing her close connection with Chailey, she wrote, taking a step back would enable her to devote her remaining years to the 'broader aspects' of its welfare.

But this surrendering of the levers of power unmistakably represented a sea change, as Dame Grace herself acknowledged: 'So ends the first chapter of Chailey, Mr Chairman,' she concluded. 'I wish all good luck to the second.'

Time had, indeed, moved on. The Heritage was now preparing for a very different world as part of the new National Health Service, and many felt that her continued involvement was a hindrance. She could hardly be expected to embrace the changes with enthusiasm. Indeed, in a letter to a friend she described it as a bitter blow, adding: 'The only argument with an east wind is to put on your overcoat – and I am trying to take the matter philosophically.' To the Bishop of London she confided: 'If I could only have definite assurance that this great educational and vocational venture here at the Heritage could go on unchanged, I should be so much happier.'

In her 'Founder's notes' in the annual report of 1947–48 she wrote: 'The feelings of many are mixed at this juncture when the old is being changed

From the 1948 Heritage book: 'The tablets in the Queen Elizabeth Home have never failed to attract the attention of visitors, showing as they do the generosity of the warm-hearted American people to those innocent little victims of the second world war.

'They also serve to remind the staff of the great debt of gratitude we all owe to the British War Relief Society Incorporated of the United States of America for championing the cause of these hapless chilren, many of whom could not have survived but for the care and attention received at the Heritage.'

A visit by the Queen and her daughters (with Princess Elizabeth on the extreme right of the picture) on June 27th 1945. The baby is being held in a Rollier swing. [Fox Photos Ltd]

into the new, and the well-beloved voluntary hospital system, which has done such magnificent work, passes into the cold hands of officialdom, or in other words those of the State.' This was hardly conciliatory language.

As those cold hands grew closer there was an urgent, sometimes acrimonious debate about the relationship between the educational and medical work at Chailey. Should the Heritage withdraw from all but peripheral medical treatment, becoming once again a school with beds attached? Should it offer a complete orthopaedic service for the area, with wards and clinics, while retaining the unique character of its educational side as (whatever the terminology should be) a 'school for cripples'?

The governors, fearing the powerful influence of the new highly-centralised health service, had approached the Ministry of Education with a request that the residential school should be separated from the hospital and become an independent residential special school: the links between school and hospital would be maintained by having a common medical staff and the same headmaster for both the residential school and the hospital school.

Murray Levick, chairman of the management committee, was strongly opposed to this idea, convinced that any separation of the two sides of the Heritage 'would destroy the efficacy of each'. Medical considerations 'must take priority when considering the welfare of handicapped school children'.

The Medical Council insisted that 'every child, whether in hospital or school, must be considered to be in the charge of the matron at all times', and it gave its reasons for this necessity 'lest the school teachers should misunderstand them'. Children with disabilities were less able to stand up to fatigue than normal children, and 'from the intellectual standpoint their supervision and handling do not come under the heading of normal psychology'. If they were troublesome the matron should be consulted before any disciplinary action was taken.

Grace Kimmins, as we might expect, had already urged that 'it was important that the educational side should not be swamped by the medical side in considering the general practice', but she was now but a single voice in a swelling debate.

Making a tactical but incomplete withdrawal, she continued to live at Chailey ('to inspire, and occasionally to goad,' as a later headmaster was to write). She was cared for at the Old Heritage by Mr and Mrs Keating ('Jim' and 'Mum' to the pupils), who had originally looked after the children at St George's. She was allowed expenses (amounting to more than £1,700 in 1947) incurred in the buying of presents for donors, the entertainment of visitors, house keeping, servants' wages and stationery. Her main financial support was provided by two annuities, each worth £1,000, purchased for her by the Heritage at a cost of nearly £8,000, at the same time as annuities totalling £2,120 had been acquired on behalf of her three servants, Lily Jones, Ernest Cook and Ellen Jones.

She had not gone, but the first chapter of Chailey had, without question, come to an end.

Under New Management

On July 5th 1948 the Heritage became part of the National Health Service under the direction of the South-East Metropolitan Regional Hospital Board. Grace Kimmins clearly, and understandably, feared that inspiration was about to be replaced by mere organisation – and it's a fact that for anyone researching the Chailey story there are far more minutes of meetings to wade through after 1948, not to speak of a continuous stream of closely (sometimes hotly) argued policy statements and initiatives. Where these involve what we might term the philosophy of the place – what it aims to provide for the children in the often conflicting areas of health and education – they often make fascinating reading, but my brief, mercifully, is to present the broad sweep of the story and in predominantly human terms. Mrs Kimmins herself would surely have agreed that the Heritage continued (and continues) to be staffed by dedicated, as well as efficient, people wishing the best for the children in their care. The wrangles have been largely over how to achieve it.

The first issue of a new magazine launched to mark the Heritage's reorganisation.

At the time of the State take-over, the scholars (now patients) at Chailey came from as many as 52 local authorities scattered across the country. The medical establishment of 22 staff included four consultant orthopaedic surgeons, three dental surgeons, two physicians to the nursing staff, two consultant paediatricians, a consultant surgeon, a consultant physician, a neurologist, a consultant oculist, a pathologist, a radiologist, an anaesthetist and an ear, nose and throat surgeon, plus the medical director and his deputy and a junior resident medical officer.

Administration required eleven officers: the headmaster and two deputies, the matron and her deputy, an administrator and assistant, an accountant, a registrar, a clerk of works and a chaplain. The Heritage also retained the professional services of an auditor, legal adviser, architect, consulting engineer and bankers.

In its final annual report in 1948, the governing body of the former voluntary institution expressed pride in its international reputation an expressed the hope that it would 'continue to flourish and develop along its own peculiarly pioneer lines'. Changes, however, were inevitable, and one in particular was strongly opposed by Mrs Kimmins: there was to be a single hospital and a single educational unit, with no division according to gender.

She must have seen it coming. In the 1948 book she included a preface by Sir Cyril Burt (professor of psychology at University College, London and honorary psychologist at the Heritage) which tackled this contentious issue head-on.

'From time to time,' he wrote, 'we hear much of the trend toward co-education, and no doubt in certain circumstances and for ordinary children such a principle has its undoubted merits. But in dealing with crippled boys and girls it is, in my view, a sound psychological principle to keep the two sexes separate during the greater part of the school period; and I may perhaps venture to hope that those who take an interest in the schools in the near future will preserve the methods which do not merely seem best on theoretical grounds, but have also been confirmed by long first-hand experience.'

It was a lost cause. It was eventually agreed that a single school of 300 children should be developed, divided equally between boys and girls, with a primary department (10–12 years) and a secondary school (up to 16 years). The existing boys' school site would be developed, with new accommodation built either in West Field or on the southern part of the Old Heritage site. St George's was to remain residential for boys, but separate accommodation for junior boys would be provided there, and its recreational facilities would be improved. Both junior and senior girls would be housed 'upon one or other of the sites adjacent to the present boys' school'. The head teacher and his staff would be responsible for out-of-school activities, while matron was responsible for their health and for the domestic arrangements.

The hospital was to have 250 orthopaedic beds (admission, isolation, recovery and staff sick bay) and 100 preventative beds, 'in order to allow economical employment of the necessary specialist medical, nursing and other staff. There were to be common theatres, X-ray and physiotherapy departments, laboratories and kitchens. These were all to be situated at the girls' heritage, but only after a vigorous debate. The architect was against the site, because the buildings would be overshadowed by the Clump, and the only way of fitting everything in was by way of 'ribbon development' – he preferred building the hospital in the south-facing West Field, so ensuring that the whole of the Heritage was on one site. The disadvantages of this site were voiced with equal strength: exposure to south-westerly gales: the consequent abandonment of existing hospital buildings at the girls' heritage, rescheduling them as residential accommodation; the lack of existing buildings to form a nucleus of the new hospital; and the large amount of clay on the site. The regional hospital board eventually decided in favour of the girls' heritage site (soon to be called the New Heritage).

The combined health and educational proposals envisaged some 650–700 places, demanding a staff of some 450, together with separate hostel accommodation for nursing and domestic staff and residential married accommodation.

Nursing recruitment at Chailey, however, was in something of a crisis.

Nurses Wanted

'Most of the staff were young, with the trained sisters to keep very strict control of us,' recalled Sheila Jeftha (née Mitchell) of her time at Chailey. She left school in 1951 to live-in at the Heritage as a probationer nurse, not being able to train properly until she was 18.

'A day started at 6.30am and ended at 6.30pm. Nights were the reverse: 10 nights on and four off. These had to be done in three-month blocks, and we had to move into the senior nurses' home. They carried on as usual, with no regard for our needing to sleep, and we could not, due to their rank, ask them to "shut up". For this we were paid £3 10s per month, all found.

'The wearing of uniform meant that we only needed a smart "going out" outfit, which was all we could afford. I tried to go home, about two hours away on the bus, about once a month, so it was a tight budget.

'I was never able to train as a nurse, as I became ill before I was 18. Looking back, this was through sheer overwork and exploitation. I was working on the ward which had the sick bay for staff attached. The nursing extended across both, so when we had a flu epidemic the workload was enormous. In fact, the sister of the ward became a patient and I, 17 years old, was in charge of the ward on several occasions. I finally succumbed to

'The comedian Jimmy Edwards lived close by and would often ride past our Warren Wood nursing quarters. We'd hear his lovely cheery voice wishing us "Good morning, nurses!" '

A nurses' photocall at the Heritage, c. 1949. [*Hamlin's News Service Ltd*]

the illness and could not shake it off for weeks. My mother then decided that I was not strong enough for such a demanding job, so I sought something easier and took a clerical post in the Middlesex Hospital.'

This sad tale of a keen recruit lost to nursing may not be typical, but it certainly has something of the flavour of the immediate post-war years at the Heritage. Life was a struggle for probationers and student nurses, who were hard pressed and poorly paid, with a system of wage differentials which created extra tension. Staff had to move between the different sites, often in appalling weather, and it was reported that they 'greatly appreciated' the provision of bicycles early in 1951.

Janet McCausland (née Brasnett) was another probationary nurse who fell victim to the conditions at Chailey, although her memories are predominantly happy ones (she was, for example, confirmed in the chapel by Bishop Bell), and she fulfilled a nursing career after her initial experience at the Heritage. She arrived from Norfolk in the autumn of 1952, at the age of 17.

'It was a real adventure for me, coming all that way to my first job. I spent months on night duty, alone in charge of a ward. It beggars belief, doesn't it?

'The atmosphere was tough, but I don't mean Dickensian. The children were cared for, but they weren't treated as cripples. There wasn't a lot of sympathy around. They were pushed to do as much as they could for themselves, and once you were imbued with the culture of the place you began to treat them as normal people. They responded very well.

All part of a nurse's duties . . . Scene from a Heritage Christmas card. [Stephanie Howe]

'The girls slept outside, however cold it might be: sometimes that winter there was a quarter of an inch of frost on the bedheads. At four o'clock every morning I had to pull them in, all by myself. I don't know why that was. With that and the constant wringing out of nappies in cold water I began to get a problem with my wrists. It got so bad that on one occasion I was shut inside my room – I didn't have the strength in my wrists to turn the door handle.

'We had to hump the girls around, and many of them were as big as I was. Nowadays that wouldn't be allowed. The nurses put up with things they wouldn't dream of today. It made me ill, and my wrists were worse and worse, so I was discharged sick. Father was summoned by matron to take me home, and that was the end of my time at the Heritage.'

Discipline was pretty tough, too. Margaret Lister Williams later remembered her time as a nurse at the Heritage at the time of nationalisation in 1948: 'I cannot imagine many of today's young people accepting a 10pm deadline to their off-duty days,' she suggested, 'and the signing-in procedure in a book kept by the head porter. Woe betide those who were rash enough or careless enough to be late in! A visit to the Matron's office would ensue.

'Everyone was much more formal 50 years ago. Consultants were regarded with awe and nurses hurried to hold doors open for them and only spoke when addressed. Things are much more relaxed now, rightly so, but never in my wildest dreams would I have expected to hear first names being used between junior medical staff and nurses when engaged in their professional roles!'

Night security was a further problem in the wilds of Chailey, and one attempt at a solution had an unhappy outcome. Various offers of labrador dogs had been made in 1948, but as the breed was regarded as too expensive to keep, the Heritage advertised for any breed that would not cost more than a pound a day. Within a month three black and white Scottish sheepdog puppies had been bought and put in the care of the head porter, who wired off a space as their playground. By the end of the year, however, they were becoming 'a little treacherous', and two years later a man was attacked and paid £1 compensation 'in respect of his trousers'. The offending animal was destroyed and replaced by a trained guard dog, but he performed no better and was eventually removed, matron deciding that she would not ask for another 'at present'.

Accommodation for residential and night staff, meanwhile, improved only gradually. In 1949 the Heritage acknowledged that finding somewhere for its resident medical officer to stay was still a problem. He was putting up 'at great expense' at the King's Head, from where he later moved to the home of Mrs Orton – the widow of a local GP, who had a tennis court which the young nurses were invited to use.

Ever since the 1948 NHS take-over, it had been recognised that training facilities for nurses were necessary at Chailey, with a single matron in charge not only of the hospital, but of the school nursing service. This reorganisation 'would enable the Heritage to apply for recognition as an affiliated training school and for the orthopaedic nursing certificate, and go far to place the Heritage in a position to attract its fair share of the available nursing staff'. In August 1948, however, it became clear that the Heritage might not be recognised 'in view of the very specialist nature of its work, which was suitable neither for a complete children's training nor for orthopaedic training, because adults were not admitted'.

The following year the matrons concerned formally proposed an alternative scheme, which would make Chailey a nurse training centre of the Mid Sussex group of hospitals: candidates (such as Sheila and Janet)

Miss Margaret Machel, a red-headed matron, was remembered in a 'fire-stained' glass window in St Helen's Chapel.

'She had the affection and admiration of her staff in spite of some rather old-fashioned rules. Any nurse who broke a Peter Rabbit nursery cup or dish was fined sixpence. Plain china was not charged. Thermometers were sixpence per breakage, too.'

'One of my sad memories was of Captain. He was a border collie, one of three given to the three centres of Chailey. St George's had Colonel, and the girls at the New Heritage had General.

'Captain was run over by, of all people, our vicar at St Martin's. I chose a few words from one of my dog books I used to read from, and a wooden plaque was made to put on his grave.'

would enter a preliminary training school or a children's long-term hospital at 17½ years of age, but would not be encouraged to take up general training until 18 years old.

Such a scheme had to await the gradual development of a corporate identity by the local group of hospitals. In the meantime, an assistant nurses training school was formed in the region, with nurses leaving at 18 to pursue their general training elsewhere. Those who wanted a training in adult orthopaedics went to Pembury Hospital over the border in Kent. In 1950 the matrons briefly considered the idea of a shortened course of nurse training for older women, but they ruled it out on the grounds that 'only older women of outstanding ability can absorb knowledge readily, and such women are unlikely to be attracted to a student nurse course'. The assistant nurse training scheme was thought to be of more practical value for this kind of candidate and, in any case, 'older women do not usually settle down in hospital'.

Although the Heritage increased its nursing staff in 1951, making it possible to admit more babies, within a few months the Ministry of Health was urging economies in all hospitals. (Chailey considered using water from the wells in order to make savings, but a sanitary inspector's critical report on the well at the Boys' Heritage put paid to that idea.) In January 1953 the ministry demanded a 5 per cent reduction in hospital staff. Not surprisingly, a Heritage recruitment drive four years later elicited a poor response: its establishment of 76 overworked staff was 20 posts short of the necessary figure for meeting its future programme.

Fortunately, at the end of 1956 (by which time a number of trained nurses offered posts at Chailey had turned them down because of the standard of residential accommodation) approval was given for a new nurses home to be built at Warren Wood. When this was eventually opened in 1958 the upper floor was occupied by the night nurses, with the senior day nurses downstairs. Staff nurses were accommodated in Warren Wood House, and the Queen Elizabeth block hostel was made available to domestic staff and nursing auxiliaries.

The problem wasn't solved overnight, but the corner had been turned.

An Inspector Calls

A 'who does what' debate was inevitable in the aftermath of the absorption of the Heritage in the National Health Service. At the beginning of 1948 the Ministry of Education had written to the Heritage stating that responsibility for both the hospital and the schools would now lie with the Ministry of Health. The latter, however, declined responsibility for the actual teaching of the children, either in the schools or in the hospital wards. A house committee was to be set up, comprising 90 per cent of the existing governors, and this would have 'reasonable autonomy with regard to day-to-day affairs'. The Ministry of Education was also in favour of this committee acting as school managers, submitting accounts to local education authorities for the full costs of education but not for the cost of maintenance of the children. The eventual upshot was that the school governors extricated themselves from nationalisation by running Chailey as a non-maintained special day school, leaving full responsibility to the NHS for all activities out of school hours.

There was, too, an anguished 'who pays for what' debate. The school managers claimed that for six months after transfer to the NHS no income had been received. Although the Ministry of Education had agreed that the school managers would be entitled to accommodation and maintenance grants, it had been assumed that one-third of their funds was made up of voluntary income.

In 1951 a report by His Majesty's Inspectors (following the first full inspection since the Education Act of 1944) gave the school size as 235 pupils (144 boys and 91 girls), of whom 89 received their education in the wards. The boys' ages ranged from 8 to 16 years and the girls' from two to 16 years. Some 48 local education authorities sponsored these children, most of whom were suffering from 'orthopaedic conditions, tuberculosis of bones and joints or cerebral palsy'. There was, the report said, 'a fairly quick turnover', with two hundred children having been discharged in the previous two years. The staffing establishment stood at 15 teachers in the boys' school and nine in the girls', and there was a 'happy corporate life and community feeling', the children displaying 'pride and loyalty for their school'.

The school day still carried some echoes of its 'men made here' past. The boys' school, with two primary and seven secondary classes, offered not only general subjects (English, arithmetic, history and geography), but handicrafts (woodwork, book binding and printing), arts and crafts, religious instruction and music. The daily timetable provided six sessions of 40–50 minutes, from 9.30–12.30 and 2–4.15.

Tony Williams, at the Heritage with polio during the early 1950s, says the education was very basic in his day, with the number of crafts on offer limited, too.

'There was no science, no chemistry, and there was no plumbing or electrics. I became a printer. We had some very old equiment, and the type was set by hand – I remember designing and setting up the service sheet for Dame Kimmins' funeral. There was no real preparation for the outside

Chailey's first occupational therapist, Jill Rockey, attended every morning from Cuckfield Hospital during the 1950s:

'In order to treat as many children in the available time, I used to have about five of varying ages, two older ones helping to teach the younger ones.

'My equipment was very primitive: an iron bedstand of average height for training from chair to bed, two old plaster tables complete with drainage holes, a card table, some ornamental garden chairs and some folding chairs with tapestry material insets.

'In the winter we had the choice of choking over the Canadian-type boiler or freezing.'

world, either. They didn't give you any counselling. When you got to school leaving age they just said Goodbye, and that was that.

'The place was altogether very old-fashioned, and I was always in trouble. It's wasn't a case of pupil power, but some of us wanted changes. Not that it did us any good – they didn't listen. We didn't like the uniform and not being allowed to wear long trousers. As for girls, I thought it would be good if we got together with them in drama productions or something like that, but meeting them was absolutely taboo!'

The girls' school was divided into two sections, since two-thirds of the children were in ward classes. The 'school' section comprised three classes (preparatory, junior, senior) and the 'hospital' three wards (nursery, junior, senior). The curriculum included general subjects, needlework and housecraft, arts and crafts, religious instruction and music. Although both sections sometimes had six periods of tuition, the 'school' timetable ran from 9.45–12.30 and 2–4, while the 'hospital' from 10–12 and 2—4.

'One day at the Heritage is very much like another' wrote a boy in the 1951 edition of *The Heritage*. 'We get up when the bell rings at 7am. We wash, get dressed and clean our boots. Breakast is at 8am, and sometimes we have egg and bacon. Then we get ready for school. We walk across the common, and after the morning service we start school in all the various

One of the two primary classes in 1953.

96

classes. We go for dinner at 12.30 until 2pm. Afternoon school is from 2 until 4.15pm. In the evening there are all sorts of things to do. Some have pets, some go to Scouts or Cubs, some play games and some do nothing. A day here is very full and I am ready for bed at 8pm.'

But not everything was rosy. The 1951 report said improvements needed to be made in both the number and – rather more damning – suitability of the school staff. The age range of the classes needed to be reduced and, significantly, craft work ought not to take such a prominent part in the curriculum of the younger children. It should 'be used to a greater extent for educational purposes, as compared with purely vocational aims.' Better facilities were required for 'backward' children, and the accommodation in general must be improved.

The Heritage's education committee responded with a number of proposals, while declaring that 'the fundamental nature of the school should not be altered'. The school would consist of a nursery class of 2–6 year-olds; a primary school of mixed classes, aged 6-11; and a secondary modern school where the children should receive a general education, 'probably in mixed classes', for the first two years, although 'craft work should take its place as an educational subject, and the children should take part in more than one craft.'

From the age of 13–14 years emphasis on craft work would be increased, although it would still be regarded as educational rather than vocational 'except possibly in certain cases where it might be considered advisable in the interests of the child to commence vocational training at an earlier age'. Thereafter the education of each child would be considered carefully 'so that some children might then take a vocational course, while others continued with their general education, with increased emphasis on craft work'. Bootmaking, for so many years a staple trade at Chailey, would not be made available to children under 14 because of the 'poor conditions attaching to this trade', but there would be courses for boys in woodwork, printing or 'commercial subjects', while the girls would learn needlework, homecraft or the aforementioned commercial subjects. Despite this stout defence of practical skills, plans to convert craft shops into classrooms were now drawn up.

After the newly-appointed county psychologist was asked to advise the Heritage on what might be done by way of vocational guidance and 'after-care', a social worker with this responsibility was appointed to liaise with local education authorities. A library and reading room were proposed, an almoner and a recreational assistant were appointed and an extensive list of out-of-school activities was drawn up: gardening, fretwork, carving, sketching, Cubs and Scouts, dramatic readings and productions, a music group, a stamp club, penfriends, games and hobbies, tournaments, a sports day, a school magazine and educational visits to places of interest.

Teachers were paid £52 a year for the 7½ hours a week they were expected to spend supervising these activities, while those who undertook further training at Brighton Technical College or who subscribed to correspondence courses would be given assistance with their fees and travel costs.

How they dealt with school-leavers in the 1930s: 'My step-father Robert Cork spent about 12 years at Chailey Heritage. At 16, never having ventured far from Chailey, and never unescorted, he was told to pack his belongings, was taken to the local railway station, given the fare to Whitstable and the address of a carpenter there, and that was the end of Chailey's involvement!'

Ian Dury, the actor, writer, lyricist and lead singer with the Blockheads, was a pupil at Chailey during the 1950s, suffering from polio. He later looked back in anger on his time at the Heritage – but he always ended any tirade by saying the if he had not been to Chailey he would not have succeeded. He died in March 2000.

Despite all these changes, Mrs Kimmins' old public school model was not entirely obsolete: under the new regime the headmaster was to introduce a house system at St George's, with a resident master for each of the three houses.

The way forward was now agreed. In 1952, four years after the Ministry of Health assumed responsibility for the hospital facilities, Chailey Heritage Craft School was recognised by the Ministry of Education as an independent hospital special school with its own body of governors. It would be some years before they were completed, but a programme of new buildings was now set in train.

An exhibition of needlework and light crafts at the Heritage in December 1954 – 'a representative display of the work produced under the direction of Miss Smith in junior and senior girls' classes and in the senior ward. The display also includes work produced in the junior mixed ward under the direction of Miss Duck.'

Fifty Years On

'When I arrived at Chailey Heritage in July 1953 there were 120 boys resident at St George's, and with St Martin's [the Old Heritage] and the New Heritage there was a grand total of around 230–240 children. There were no day pupils and no wheel chairs allowed, except for a few on the hospital wards, but *not* for individual use. The expectation was that all might be taught to walk.'

So begins a memoir by Dr Michael Strode, the much-loved resident medical officer who worked at Chailey until 1988. He arrived in the Heritage's golden jubilee year, an anniversary which seems not to have been marked with any of the founder's customary razzamatazz.

Soon after he arrived, Dr Strode began taking a few Chailey children to Lourdes, in association with the Handicapped Children's Pilgrimage Trust. Children from all over Britain took part and were divided into groups of ten, with a helper for each child: each group had its own leader and nurse, with a doctor caring for a number of the groups in the hotels. Children from Chailey were mixed in with groups from other places and they were also clamouring to go again, the trips being regarded as a holiday as well as a pilgrimage. Later, in the 1970s, he took four juniors to Caldy each year for a beach holiday – a gift from the Cistercian monastery there, with the excitement for the children of the crossing to the island in an open boat.

He worked under Dr Philip Quibell, who had become medical administrator in 1950 (he never forgot the daunting experience of being interviewed by Mrs Kimmins) and was to serve the Heritage for 25 years, latterly as consultant paediatrician. Dr Quibell oversaw the development of medical and therapeutic expertise which led to Chailey becoming a renowned centre for the treatment of children with multiple disabilities. He had many international contacts, was widely admired for his approach to the rehabilitation of handicapped children and was in 1976 presented with the OBE in recognition of his work for the disabled both at the Heritage and elsewhere.

'When I started at Chailey,' he said on this retirement, 'I felt the first things I had to do were to get the equipment up to an adequate level and give some kind of planning guide.

'In those days the cure for TB, the prevalent disease, was still sunlight and fresh air, and many still slept in the open. There was little physiotherapy, no speech or occupational therapist, clinical pathologist or experimental workshop.'

In 1955 Dr Quibell (affectionately known as 'Q') would hold the first functional assessment conference, with the idea that everyone concerned with the care of a child should meet regularly and discuss the physical handicaps and emotional problems on an all-round basis. These conferences, which gave much thought to the future of school leavers, were widely copied.

The kinds of disablement treated at the Heritage were to change dramatically during its second half-century.

Dr Strode's kindness was legendary, and radiographer Janet Darby gives an example of it:

'Each child was a challenge to X-ray, and as the years progressed and the type of disabilities changed, more help was needed, but someone was always prepared to lend a hand.

'Many times there were children who were really frightened of having an X-ray, and we often spent a full half-hour or more carrying the child in and reassuring them before we could proceed.

'Dr Strode's never-ending store of patience was invaluable.'

'Dr Quibell virtually lived on site in one of the cottages near to the Old Heritage,' recalls Janet Darby. 'He was therefore present morning, noon and night, taking all the decisions which were needed to help the children and to enable the Heritage to run smoothly.

'He even authorised me to have my springer spaniel in the X-ray department on the grounds that he would help the children get over their fear of coming for an X-ray. He was right – and Scruff became a much-loved member of staff for the next 15 years.'

'He always had time for everyone, big or small. I found one child on Coxen house quite upset one day as a favourite toy was broken but, smiling between the tears, the child said "Dr Quibell will mend it this evening"'.

'The four main groups of disability,' wrote Dr Strode of his first days at Chailey, 'were surgical tuberculosis, post poliomyelitis, cerebral palsy and congenital abnormalities, including a number of limb deficiencies, and one boy with spina bifida.

'The atmosphere on the medical side was distinctly orthopaedic: plaster casts and proning cases for those with TB of the spine; protective splints for TB of the hips and knees; calipers, crutches and spinal jackets for the casualties of poliomyelitis; and physiotherapy for those with cerebral palsy and for all who needed it – the majority. Open-air nursing was still in vogue, even in Princess Elizabeth Clinic, our babies ward.'

At this time the children were divided between six ward areas on the New Heritage site, depending upon their age and ability. Adjoining each ward was a schoolroom where the children did their lessons: they then returned to the ward to eat and sleep. During the day children would often need to leave lessons for a variety of reasons, among them physiotherapy or x-ray examinations. There was an obvious benefit in being able to do everything on one site, rather than having to visit a local hospital. Children at the Old Heritage site lacked this convenience, of course, since they had to make frequent journeys to the medical facilities, but every effort was made to keep the disruption of their day to a minimum.

There was a small operating theatre at the New Heritage, and children from the Old Heritage were often allocated to a New Heritage ward during their convalescence: their bed could be wheeled into the schoolroom so that their education wasn't interrupted.

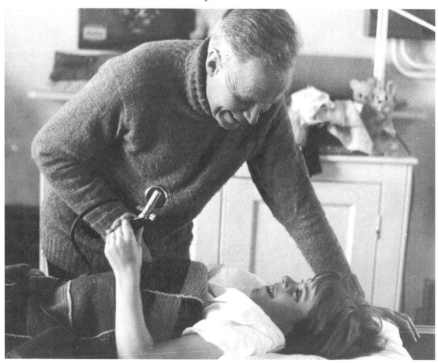

Smiles all round: Dr Strode had a wonderful bedside manner. [Janet Darby]

Amazing Grace

May 6th 1870 – March 3rd 1954

Grace Kimmins, created a Dame of the British Empire in 1950 for her lifetime of commitment to handicapped children, was still in residence at the 50-year mark, although she had been in ill health for some time. Her death the following year brought a crop of warm obituaries and reminiscences, including this in the Lancet:

'Dame Grace was a dictator, she had to be, and she had some of the defects of a dictator. But she had the hallmark of fine greatness, a divine sense of humour, and could, and did, laugh at herself. A goddess with a chuckle – truly, a great woman gone from us.'

Another memoir in the Lancet recalled the years of her retirement 'when she seemed small and frail, but with a fertile and active mind, still planning, still voicing her views with a forthright incisive manner. When her health allowed, she would attend the services at the boys' chapel in her wheeled chair, indomitable as ever, still anxious to see her growing family. Shrewd in her judgement of people, with the manner and way of the great impressario, she belonged to the generation of individualists.'

Those present at her memorial service, including representatives of Buckingham Palace, heard her described as 'one of the greatest English women of the twentieth century' and the Heritage as 'still the most famous in the world as the public school of crippledom'.

A later article in the Times, in which the reporter admitted to a nervousness when interviewing such a 'legendary figure', told how 'during the next hour or two of the interview she talked without ceasing about the needs of the maimed and helpless and how they must be trained to serve their country by doing useful work.

'What the handicapped did not want, she said, was sentimental pity; what they urgently required was help after leaving the Heritage and serving, perhaps, in some sheltered workshop.

'Yet she was not slow to appreciate the fresh problems perpetually created by the changing pattern of disease. The last time I saw her she spoke of the importance of treating crippled babies as early as possible, and of the need for more after-care when the severely disabled went out into the world.'

Olive Fraser, nurse 1927–30:
'My memory is of Dame Grace walking, or should I say sailing, over the common, in her blue dress, grey cloak and winged cap.

'She always had a word and a smile for us, and if we happened to be looking tired she would creep behind matron and whisper: "Never stand when you can sit; never sit when you can lie" – upsetting matron's authority.'

H.W. Leggatt, former teacher:
'Dame Grace Kimmins sent for me and another young master to go to her in the council chamber. We braced ourselves for the worst. When we arrived she said to my colleague: "You remind me of a winter's apple, but whether you improve with keeping or not we shall have to wait and see".'

The 14-year-old Michael Baldock was put in a so-called 'hip spica' to lock his hip in place.

'It extended from my knees to my chest – a sort of plaster cast. I got around on crutches. The pin they put in lasted for twenty years'

Elaine Baldock, nursing at Chailey at that time, remembers that there was an iron bar across the front of the spica', and this was held by staff in order to help the children move about.

'It was very heavy plaster in those days,' she says, 'not today's light-weight material. Some of the girls I was nursing lay for years in what you might call plaster beds. They were laid on their stomachs and the plaster was moulded to their bodies around them. They had to wait for it to set hard. It formed a shell, with an opening at the top. They could be lifted out occasionally for a blanket bath, but they couldn't move.'

Michael's younger brother Brian was at the Heritage from about three years old, suffering from a congenital dislocation of the hip, and his worst memories are of the days when his plaster had to be changed.

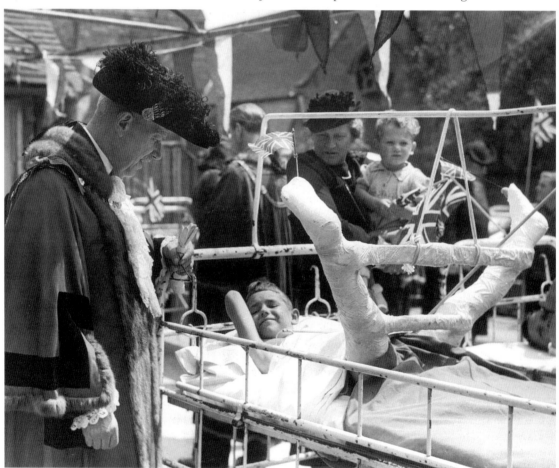

Making the best of it: a young lad encased in plaster in so-called 'frog position' manages a smile for the visiting Lord Mayor of London. [*Keystone Press Agency*]

'They would wheel me on a trolley to the plaster room, where I would scream the place down because of my memories of the last visit. I had plaster from just under my armpits down to just above my knees, and they had to cut if off with an enormous pair of silver plier-like cutters. When the hinges closed they would pinch your skin, and I would have a series of pinch-marks all down one side after the plaster was taken off.

'Then I would have to have the new one put on, which was warm and clammy, turning cold and clammy. It would stick to your skin for a couple of days until it eventually dried, and would then make you itch like mad. You'd be frantic to find something long and thin enough to poke down the plaster to scratch the itch, and as soon you scratched one itch another one would start somewhere else.'

Barbara McCabe (née Scott) has similar memories of the 'horrific' cutters: 'I used to scream, and they would give me a whole tin of Smarties to pacify me. I think it was the terror rather than any actual pain.

'I had dislocated hips, and I was plastered in the frog position. My feet used to be out of the bed, and because of the cold they put women's bedsocks on me stuffed out with cotton wool.'

Her memories of life at Chailey during the 1950s and early 1960s are predominantly happy ones, however, including the regular Sunday procession around the site of two donkeys. Visiting was now allowed every weekend, and the education, she says, was good.

Doreen Quibell, a sister at the Heritage during the 1950s, remembers the cumbersome gear some of the children had to wear.

'TB was common in those days, and the last TB spine I saw was in a two-year-old in the mid-Fifties who was treated in Brighton and moved to Chailey later. The antibiotic treatment for TB was only just coming in.

'Children with TB spines at Chailey came in when they were very young. Most had to wear apparatus like spinal jackets. Some had bilateral hip splints and jackets, which they hated. The biggest misery a child could be asked to put up with was the Fisher jacket, which held them rigid from their hips to their knees to their shoulders. They were made by Mr Florence, the appliance maker, who was at Chailey from 1947 until 1960. [His son, John, would become the official orthotist in 1975: see page 123.] They had metal frames covered with padding and chamois leather. The bilateral ones had metal rods to keep the hips abducted with pads.

'New patients were nursed on a metal trolley with a wooden tray, like a baker's tray, on which a block was fixed across at the level of the child's kyphos [a spinal curve]. This was covered by a horse-hair mattress. The aim was to straighten the kyphos by exerting pressure until the TB was quiescent, as judged by X-rays.

'X-rays were taken at intervals, to check activity. The X-ray technician was Corporal Hayes. He had been at Chailey as a returned soldier during the first world war, living in the huts near St George's. He trained to take X-rays and continued for many years.

'When did they dispense with jackets? Many continued to wear them until adulthood, as they had marked deformities and needed the support. Also, the TB could become active again, or cause TB meningitis, which was

Sister Harrison, in charge of the ambulant girls' dormitory, was known as 'our Chailey mum' by the girls.

'She helped them nurse damaged rooks back to health when they were shot in the Clump. Such birds were general pets until they chose to fly away. On Rennie ward a swallow that was found on the ground was fed with dead flies and tiny bits of suitable food at intervals: the titbit was pushed down its gullet with an orange stick. This pet also finally took wing, although it had needed devoted round-the-clock care from baby to feathers.'

often fatal. There was a committee which decided which children to treat, as there was a very small supply of antibiotics. Only children who had a chance to recover were treated.'

Mrs Quibell recalls cases of osteomyelitis, which caused bad deformities of the bones, with legs sometimes being amputated to prevent further spread of infection: artificial limbs were made at Roehampton. Children with birth deformities such as Apert's Syndrome were very difficult to feed because of their abnormal palates. Little children with polio were transferred to Chailey mainly from the Dartford Fever Hospital.

'They were considered to still be infectious, and as Chailey was not on main drainage at this time the disinfectant used upset the septic tank. Main drainage was put in around the end of the 1950s.'

During his 25 years at Chailey Dr Philip Quibell (affectionately known as 'Q'), oversaw the development of medical and therapeutic expertise which led to the Heritage becoming a renowned centre for the treatment of children with multiple disabilities.

After the acute phase, some of the polio victims were unable to breathe properly when they were sleeping, and there was a respirator that could be used if necessary. Many had severe paralysis and curvatures of the spine. Children with polio often suffered from chilblains, and cod liver oil cream would be rubbed into their limbs. Many of them wore calipers, but those able to go to school wore the school uniform. Life, after all, was to continue as normally as humanly possible.

A number of honorary consultants would come down to the Heritage for Saturday morning clinics, thus giving the children the benefit of some of the country's top specialist expertise. Staff, moreover, were expected to give up their Saturday mornings to provide the necessary back-up.

'Babies and toddlers were admitted from London via Dr Pinkney, who was the consultant paediatrician at the time,' says Doreen Quibell. 'They also came from the Invalid Children's Aid Association. They had a mixture of conditions – for example, Pink Disease, caused by mercury teething powder. They were very miserable and had no appetite. Some babies had what was called 'marasmus', really a symptom of malnutrition. These were babies who, after the war, were living in poor housing, with insufficient sunlight and stimulation. They were often fat, pasty and anaemic, and they were undeveloped socially. They responded to the diet, stimulation and fresh air and were able to return home.'

Elaine Baldock, a nurse at the Heritage in the early 50s, says 'I would not have missed my two years at Chailey for the world'. Many of the children had terrible disabilities, 'but those children had some of the most wonderful natures I have ever met. God made some wonderful and brave children, gifted with something that other children weren't. I shall always remember them, their cuddles, their smiles, above all their bravery.'

Another nurse, Sylvia Vine (née Ginger), has similarly fond memories of working for two years at the Heritage from late 1959 as a trainee.

'Part of it was the camaraderie,' she recalls. 'We were young things, and the children themselves were such fun. Of course it was tough in many respects, and physically hard for the nurses, carrying the youngsters about. If it snowed on night duty we would bring the beds in, but I remember how freezing it felt during the winter, especially at St George's where I had a stint looking after the lads. When we bathed the little children the water was only just lukewarm, and there was no central heating or anything like that. We'd dunk them in there, but they never complained – they were used to it, and they must have become very hardy.

'I went on to have children of my own, but I can honestly say these were the happiest two years of my life.'

Roy Moules (1947–53) remembers: 'Being away from home was nothing new to me as I had spent most of my short life away from home, in and out of hospital. It was a pleasure to be in the company of other children with deformities similar to mine.

'On my first weekend at Chailey Mr Holgate asked me if I could play cricket. I soon became a regular on the school team.'

F.A. Duligall: 'The only record I could find of my existence at Chailey were the cricket scores still preserved in the library in one of the old buildings. It appears I scored at least one six at cricket. I don't know how I ran, though.'

Among other extra-curricular activities at Chailey:

Tony Harper in Heritage News, autumn 1971:
'For the third year running Chailey sent a team to compete in the Stoke Mandeville Games for the Disabled. We had entered for table tennis, snooker, running, archery and swimming.

'At dinner time [on the second day] the medals were presented. Between us we won five gold medals and one silver.'

Pam Tidy in Heritage News, summer 1979:
'The riding group has now been running successfully for over 18 months. We started with six children, and to date 27 children have been able to ride. Five of them have passed their first Riding for the Disabled Association tests.'

Chailey had its own Scout, Cub, Guide and Brownie sections, run on a voluntary basis, and many of the children spent the first week of their summer holiday at camp. Volunteers of all ages helped to run these camps, and staff gave their personal spare time, too.

Peter Ford helped set up the Scout troop, together with Bob Waller, Bernie Wren and Phil Emery:

'Ernest "Pa" Stanger, the Assistant County Commissioner for Handicapped Scouts (who was himself disabled after a motorcycle accident) was asked if it would be possible to start a group at the Heritage. He was also Group Scout Leader of the 1st Hove Scout group.

'We arranged to meet the boys, and discussed with them what scouting was all about. They were all very enthusiastic, and we soon had a Scout troop up and running. We had to meet on Saturday afternoons, as we were working during the week.

'There were between 12 and 15 boys each week. We had to slightly modify some of the tests to suit a particular boy, but they were all determined to do each test "by the book". The Wolf Cubs (as they were called in those days) were started by the 6th Hove Scout Group under Ron Pumfrey, assisted by two lady scouters.

'As far as I can remember the group was started in the 1950s and was soon registered at Scout headquarters in London. The boys had to choose what colour neckerchief to wear. This was quickly decided. It was to be the same as the 1st Hove: red and grey, representing a camp fire flame and ash.

'After a while other groups from the Hove and Portslade district were helping at the Heritage. We all agree that it was one of the most rewarding things that any of us had ever done.'

The Guides and Brownies had a longer pedigree at Chailey. In the Coming of Age book of 1924 we read that 'the Princess Louise Own Heritage Girl Guides and Brownies are second to none in smartness, alertness and all those qualities for which the Guide movement stands.' At that time they were pleased to have a hut of their own, but in 1931, thanks to the generosity of the Divisional Commissioner Miss Helen Hett, a new headquarters, 'Pax Est', was built – designed by her brother L. Keir Hett.

Hilda Ashcroft was one of the first recruits – and one of many to have fond memories of the experience.

'The ambition of every Guide was to gain so many proficiency badges that there was no more room on her sleeve, and I got further than anyone else.

'I even gained my swimming badge by swimming fifty yards with one arm. I'd learned to float during the summer holidays and one year, when Ernie happened to be on leave, he took me to the beach for a bathe. He stood by me in the water while I tried an experiment, using my good arm like the paddle of a canoe. I was doing well when Ernie said "Here, hang on. I'm getting out of my depth", and I realised I could actually swim, if only on my back. At last I had achieved something on my own.'

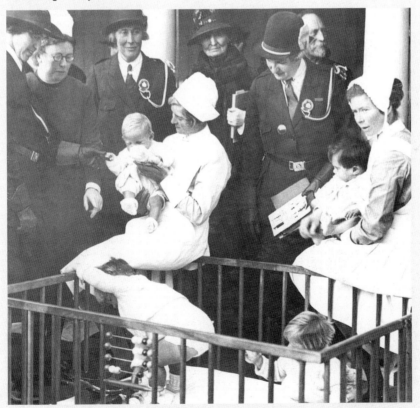

Lady Baden Powell, Chief Guide of all the World, on one of her several visits to Chailey. [Alfieri Picture Service]

Heritage News report, 1978: 'Once again a party of nine Heritage children and three adults spent a thrilling and exhausting week at Hindleap Warren Activity Centre on Ashdown Forest.

'This annual winter expedition is made possible by financial help from the Hale Trust, and we were fortunate this year to be able to met many of our benefactors when they came one day for lunch. They were able to see for themselves the enthusiasm and happiness of the children and hear first-hand descriptions of their activities.

'As usual it is the assault course which provokes most speculation beforehand, and most self-congratulation and back-slapping after the event.'

The Star of Bethlehem

Members of Grace Kimmins' family would have known better than to interfere in her running of the Heritage, but they certainly gave it their support, as they have continued to do to this day. Tony Medhurst, a Heritage boy in the 1930s, remembers her husband, Dr Kimmins ('We used to call him Narny, and her nickname was Kimbo') turning up at the hospital ward.

'He would visit us every Sunday and read the Sunday newspapers to us, particularly the sports pages – especially if there had been a Joe Louis or Tommy Farr bout.'

The Kimminses' sons were trustees of the Heritage, and Anthony was to write a Christmas play which was repeated year after year until recent times: *The Star of Bethlehem*. One of the first naval pilots in the Fleet Air Arm, who performed the original deck-landing tests and delayed parachute drops, he was also a writer and film director. His daughter, Verena Hanbury, wrote an article in the Spring 1978 issue of *Heritage News*, explaining how he had come to write it.

Lights! Verena Hanbury behind the scenes at Christmas 1965.

'When the Heritage became split by the Ministries of Health and Education my father felt that there might be a danger of the school and hospital drawing apart from each other. So he wrote a play to be performed every Christmas by children and adults from all departments, hoping that this would help to secure the spirit of unity that his mother had created with the founding of the Heritage in 1903.

'As he devoted much of his life to writing, this was a part of himself he could give to the Heritage. After many consultations with the bishop, and much study of his bible, he completed the most beautifully simple and dignified version of the Christmas story for production in St Martin's Chapel and to be performed by Heritage children – the perfect ambassadors for this story of strength and faith. Occasionally he strayed a little from the original text in order to avoid too many changes of scene which might detract from the colour and dignity of an act of worship. The words are so simple that it has been rightly pointed out that some of the teaching is missing, but the brilliance of his writing lies in its simplicity, and this is why any child can perfectly deliver any line in the play.

Sue Sumpter remembers: 'I first met Captain Kimmins when we began rehearsals for the Nativity play. He had written the play and was going to direct it.

'His most outstanding and impressive virtue was his patience in accepting us as we were. He never lost his temper or raised his voice. Evidently he did not expect Sir Laurence Oliviers and Shirley Temples, and if something was not right, he patiently went over and over it until it was satisfactory.

'Not only was he an influence in the Nativity play, but also in the school generally. He took a keen interest in what went on at Chailey, often came to the service on Sundays and always turned out to umpire the Staff v. School cricket match.'

Anthony Kimmins

'When he had written the script he asked me, as I was stage managing in London at the time, to do this production with him. As I wasn't then on any of the committees at Chailey, I was overjoyed to have the opportunity to get involved. The lighting plot proved fun, because we decided that if any member of the cast found it difficult to follow a visual or word clue they could instead follow a light, because with strong lamps in a small place you can either see or feel them. The result is that every move is slightly anticipated by a light cue which enables any child to take part.

'The play was first performed in December 1962, with my father producing and assisted by Miss Bruce. There was great support from all corners of the colony. He was very touched by everyone's enthusiasm. Not long after that first Christmas my father became ill, and by the following year he was unable to produce the play again. He asked his assistant producer Margaret Bruce to take over, which she did with outstanding sensitivity, and she has continued to reproduce something of which he would have been extremely proud.

'Since then we have continued with many laughs and a few tears, some of which were shed last year with the loss of Mr Leggatt, who arranged the music for the play and made the choir such a vital part of the whole production. There is no doubt that my father's intended message of hope and happiness and love comes out of the chapel at the end of each performance.'

Exchange reported in Heritage News:
Padre – 'Now, who can tell me what gifts the Wise Men brought?'
Stuart Lunt – 'Gold, frankenstein and myrrh.'

CHRISTMAS PARTIES AT THE HERITAGE

Christmas parties were treats involving everyone in the organisation, from top to bottom. Each ward was decorated with the full panoply of Christmas decorations, and individually wrapped, thoughtfully chosen, presents were prepared for each child. This was carried out principally by nurses and teachers – with love, affection and a massive commitment of their own time.

'Anthony Kimmins gave each nurse a handbag and her individual present,' recalled Olive Fraser. 'Mine was a long chain of squeezed out oranges with a note: "Never go short of your vitamin C". I hadn't realised how folk noticed that when preparing the children's orange juice I always sucked the skins!'

At a later period the rehabilitation unit staff would make a chariot for Father Christmas with a different theme each year. This was driven through the wards to each party in turn, accmpanied by all the rehabilitation staff and driven by Father Christmas – who for many years was Bert the storeman. As it arrived at the door of each ward the nurses would load the presents on board, and it would then be driven to the centre of the room to be distributed to the excited children.

'All the staff from round the Heritage would try to get to as many of the parties as possible,' remembers radiographer Janet Darby, 'and Philip Quibell made quite sure that he attended each and every one, no matter what other priorities awaited his attention.

'It was at times like this that Chailey really felt like one big family.'

A tense moment by the manger: Karen Seidlar and Marion Sansom in the 1965 production.

In the same issue of *Heritage News* it was reported that the play had passed its fiftieth performance the previous Christmas.

'Every year it is essentially the same (though older afficionados regret the passing of that marvellous procession up the aisle with the donkey and the children bearing gifts) and yet every year it is different. There is always some moment of totally unexpected poignancy which leaves the emotional defences hopelessly down – the arrival of the shepherd boy, the rejection at the inn, the compassion of the innkeeper's wife, the spine-chilling terror of Herod and his military police.'

After Mr Leggatt's death the music was taken over by Clifford Dann, who, Verena Hanbury recalls, 'played the organ magnificently', and the play continued to be performed for many years. It would, alas, be impossible to mount it today, the accommodating of so many wheelchairs being not the least difficulty, but back in the 1960s the Heritage certainly needed to promote as much togetherness as it possibly could. The strains were showing.

Heritage News: 'People will continue to argue whether Peter or Abu was a more toweringly impressive King, or who was the most authoritative Angel Gabriel, but the overall picture of absolute sincerity, of high professionalism remains indisputable.'

Kevin Smart demonstrates some new equipment to Sir Edward Boyle, Secretary of State for Education, with headmaster Harry Browning in the background. [Evening Argus]

Learning to the Fore

*I*n July 1964 Sir Edward Boyle, the Secretary of State for Education, opened two blocks of new classrooms at the Heritage, the culmination of four years of building work. This created, said headmaster Harry Browning, 'virtually a new school'.

At this time the Heritage Craft School had 200 children on its roll, half of them being taught in classrooms in the Old Heritage and the other half in the hospital wards at the New Heritage. The new buildings, two-thirds of the cost being met by a Ministry of Education grant, included a science laboratory, an art room, a woodwork/metalwork room and four general purpose classrooms.

In his speech, Mr Browning was enthusiastic about the latest technology: an automatic tape deck on which teachers recorded BBC school broadcasts; an ingenious machine called Possum in the commercial subjects room which allowed children to operate an electric typewriter even if they had only limited finger movements; and typists' chairs in the woodwork/metalwork room which enabled boys with poor legs to use both hands for their work.

Programme for the opening of the new school blocks.

Despite this bullish appraisal, however, the direction in which the Heritage was moving was now open to serious question. What was its chief function? Children were admitted to Chailey as hospital patients, but did this create an inbuilt bias against satisfactory education? In September 1962 there had been a meeting between representatives of the Ministry of Education, the regional hospital board, the hospital management committee, the school governors and the Chailey house committee. An assistant secretary at the Ministry of Education, Miss H.E. Clinkard, was in the chair.

'In her opening remarks,' read the minutes of this meeting, 'Miss Clinkard referred to the unique position of the Heritage, as part of it compared more nearly to a residential special school than to a hospital special school. The organisation raised certain problems which could only be overcome by the closest possible cooperation between the hospital and school authorities.'

The ministry had encouraged and assisted the governors in a policy of modernising the school, and 'it was the feeling of the ministry that when the programme was complete the greatest possible use should be made of the teaching facilities.'

Although the children being admitted to the Heritage were more severely handicapped than previously, it was argued, there was a need to improve residential accommodation so that they could be removed from the wards if medically fit, even though they were confined to wheelchairs. It had recently been agreed that a 'villa' would be built at the Old Heritage for up to 25 severely handicapped children, and it should be possible for them to attend school in the classroom. As far as possible 'the children should be

Foreword by Harry Browning in the school magazine, 1965: 'The 1960s have been full of change at Chailey. And yet, the Heritage is in essence unaltered! Its main purpose is still to encourage the development of independence, so that we spurn unnecessary help and strive to make the best possible use of the strength and intelligence with which we are blessed.'

given the benefit of the more normal life obtainable in residential accommodation rather than remaining in the more restricted confines of a hospital ward'.

The battle of wills between the medical and educational forces at Chailey was evident in the following threat: 'Miss Clinkard emphasised the importance attached by her Ministry to the upgrading of the children's residential accommodation, and intimated that if it were not possible for the hospital authorities to allocate money for this purpose it might be necessary to consider a drastic administrative reorganisation affecting the residential side of the Heritage.'

It was agreed that efforts should be 'resumed' to bring about a joint meeting between the Ministry of Health and the Ministry of Education and other interest parties. This suggests a dragging of heels which was to continue literally for years. When the house committee, the school governors and the medical staff committee gathered in May 1964, they read the minutes referred to above and reported that 'although efforts had been made locally to bring about this meeting, it had not taken place'.

When the same bodies met again in February 1965, it was reported that 'an approach by the hospital management committee to the regional hospital board urging that a joint meeting be held had been acknowledged by the senior medical officer, who proposed to visit Chailey on March 5th 1965 to discuss future policy'.

This meeting also considered the current types of diseases and congenital conditions at Chailey, noting that there was a waiting list, especially for younger spina bifida children. Tuberculosis had declined 'to such an extent that it requires no special thought'. Poliomyelitis, since the advent of the vaccine, had also shown ' a very striking fall, and is unlikely to produce any big numerical group in the future'.

Spina bifida accounted for the largest group, with 62 cases, followed by cerebral palsy (48), polio (34) and a range of other congenital conditions (32). If the present policy at the Heritage was maintained, the two largest groups would be cerebral palsy 'and the malformations'.

The most sensational of those malformations had first been noticed in 1962, and Chailey was already in the forefront of responding to it.

Thalidomide

*I*t was at the end of the 1950s that babies throughout the world – some 12,000 in all – began to be born with deformed or non-existent limbs, brain damage, eye and ear defects, damage to the nervous system and severe internal defects of the heart, kidneys, genitals and digestive tract. By 1962 390 deformed babies had been born in Britain within the space of three years, and more than 300 of them were still alive. The cause of their cruel affliction was man-made – the drug Thalidomide, prescribed for pregnant mothers as a treatment for morning sickness.

The response at Chailey was a striking throwback to the days of Dame Grace. For one thing, a titled lady was at the helm of a fund-raising appeal: Lady Hoare, wife of the lord mayor of London, took up the cause as her charity. For another, the Heritage was in the forefront of ground-breaking research into ways of helping the youngsters cope with their problems.

In October 1962 the *Daily Telegraph* reported that 'an experimental centre where the most modern artificial limbs can be made for

Lady Hoare at the opening of the workshop which was named after her. [*Sussex Express*]

Thalidomide, a synthetic module first discovered in Germany in 1954, was used to prevent morning sickness in pregnant women. Although it was withdrawn when its horrific effects were revealed, it is today re-emerging for use in other applications.

'I used to tell them: You can do two things when people come to get you out of bed in the morning. You can smile, or you can put your tongue out at them. If you smile they'll do anything for you, but if you put out your tongue, the day will go wrong.'

Danny High presents a carved bowl to Princess Margaret, who opened the experimental workshop. [*Sussex Express*]

They were a lively and loveable lot – and when they became teenagers they were quite a handful.'

Mary Sheppard arrived at the Princess Elizabeth babies ward as a nurse in 1962:

'To obtain a normal sitting position, plaster of Paris flower pots were made to fit each individual child. The pots were then put on a small wooden nursery chair mounted on casters, with a tray attached for play purposes.

'In those days we seldom went beyond Chailey Common and the surrounding lanes, and the highlight of the day was a walk across the common with as many as four or five babies, all in their flower pots, in one pram.'

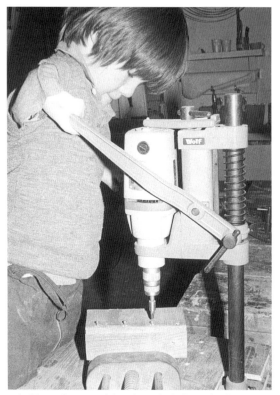

Children damaged by the Thalidomide drug often proved to be extremely resourceful.

Thalidomide victims is to be the main object of the Lady Hoare Thalidomide Fund. It is to be developed at Chailey Heritage Craft School and Hospital, East Sussex.'

The new intake was to bring an unexpected gust of fresh, positively bracing, air to the Heritage.

'It was an interesting period,' recalls Verena Hanbury, 'because the children were very bright. They had massive extra problems, because they knew why they were so badly disabled, and so of course there was an element of blame – attached to the mother sometimes. They were quite unhappy, confused children in a way.'

In the early days there was little being done elsewhere for severely handicapped children such as those who were appearing at Chailey. The advent of Thalidomide presented a completely new set of treatment problems, and all the medical disciplines had to develop new ways of helping children to adjust to their limb deficiences.

John Roberts was one of the 60 children who were brought to Chailey as babies and who spent their childhood at the Heritage. Today a married man who talks fluently, rides a bike, drives a 4x4 automatic car and includes fishing among his hobbies, he was born without ears and had a number of other physical disabilities which have necessitated around 40 operations in the first 40 years of a life which was once expected barely to reach adulthood. Immensely grateful for what Chailey did for him, he remembers some of the hardships, as well.

In July 1969 the High Court judge Mr Justice Hinchcliffe came to inspect the Heritage in order to assess the scale of damages that should be awarded to two (non-Chailey) Thalidomide children – deciding on a figure of £52,000 for a limbless child and £32,000 for one with no arms. At about this time the Chailey contingent had to be assessed, too, and John recalls the humiliation.

'You were known by your number – I was no. 14 – and you were made to take your clothes off and walk naked down a corridor and into a room full of doctors. This happened over four separate days: "Here's no. 14

coming in." When you got inside they pulled you about and prodded you. It was like some German experiment, sorting you into groups: I was about 7 years old at the time.'

After a few years in the hospital at the New Heritage, he moved to accommodation close to the chapel at the Old Heritage, and thence to St George's when he was older.

'I had no hearing at all when I was born. They were experimenting with hearing aids. I began with something called a bone conductor, which was strapped to me with a bright red headband, but I was too young for it. I switched to headphones, which improved my hearing by 17 per cent. There were seven of us in the deaf unit.'

John was given a pair of false ears in order to give him a 'normal' appearance, and they were stuck on with double-sided tape. They were realistic, but seemed pale when – thanks to the Chailey outdoor ethic – his face became tanned.

'I would play football. You should have seen their faces if someone kicked the ball at me and one of my ears came off!'

Many of the children could use their feet, and would eat with their toes. John followed suit, until his feet were tied together to encourage him to use his hands.

THE BRA FUND

Karen Smith was in Rennie Ward from 1969 to 1979, a period during which there was a quiet but warmly welcomed clothing revolution.

'Many of the girls found the uniforms difficult to put on, difficult to wear and not very flattering because of the nature of their disabilities. The sewing room helped by producing pinafore dresses with front zips, and Velcro revolutionised the 'button' down the front of the shirt. Ties eventually bit the dust, for which there was universal gratitude. Summer dresses in pretty prints, again easy to put on and wear, came after. At weekends the girls relaxed into their own clothes. Eventually uniforms were abandoned, first for the pupils and then for the staff.

'But there was a problem: many of the girls had insufficient help from home, and when the time came for them to wear bras, there was no money to purchase them. They were not on the list of 'hospital clothing' which could be supplied. Therefore the 'bra fund' was started by keeping back part of the money visitors contributed for their tea and biscuits on Sunday afternoons. The money should have been returned to the catering department, but we persuaded them we had very few and ungenerous visitors!

'This system kept the girls 'fully supported' until the hospital authority could be persuaded to pay. The system was then used for deodorants – again, not something initially on the supplies list.'

'Once a year you had a kind of MOT test. You had to strip down for an X-ray, have a blood sample taken, be measured and prodded about and photographed. Your feet would be put in warm water so that the veins would stand out, and they would inject a dye. I didn't like one doctor who was very cold and matter-of- fact, but Dr Strode was very nice and he always did it in a fun way.'

'I was amused to read in the press a former pupil complaining about her treatment as a child at Chailey Heritage – she had been sent to bed without any tea following some misdemeanour. My thoughts were "How marvellous that she was treated normally," as in those unenlightened days many of us were sent to bed without tea as punishment for our crimes.'

There is no getting away from the fact that the Thalidomide children could be a stroppy lot. On one occasion they did a bunk, finding their way to the King's Head, and being brought back to the Heritage only after downing a few glasses of cider. On another occasion they rebelled.

'We organised a demonstration,' says John, 'and insisted that the chaplain warden, Tom Galletly, come to see us. We made a lot of demands.

'Our food was awful. I suppose it was because of the cost, but while the other children at the Heritage had Marmite, peanut butter and Shreddies for breakfast, all we had was porridge every day. That was one complaint: the food was rubbish.

'Another was that we were fed up with being treated as patients. That's what they called us, but we didn't like that. And then there was the uniform. Some of us were going home at weekends, and we didn't see why we should have to dress up like that every day. We wanted a life.

'They were very shocked. They suddenly realised that we were capable of organising a meeting and making those demands. We were very independent. And we got most of those things eventually. The people in charge became carers, and there was less of a hospital feeling. I honestly believe they learned a lot from us. Things began to change.'

For Louise Medus (née Mason) they changed far too late. She came to Chailey at the age of 17 weeks in 1962 and left in September 1979. Her complaints are legion, although she puts them in an historical perspective. Some Heritage children went on to university, but Louise certainly felt that she lacked encouragement.

'The education was very poor. I came out with hardly any qualifications. Their idea was to teach you the basic English and arithmetic, but above all to make you independent. They always said there was no such word as Can't. You had to use your imagination to find ways of doing things for yourself. I was taught to write, but there was no thought that I should have a proper education. When I left Chailey I went to college and passed loads of exams, and now I lecture on the history of disability.

'Most of what was wrong with Chailey in those days was the fault of society. If you compare what it

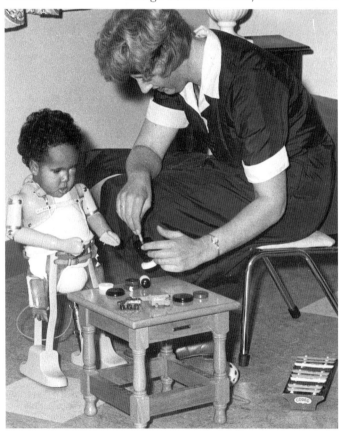

Andrew Maull with occupational therapist, Miss Ransome. Those artificial limbs were 'state of the art' in 1963. [Sussex Express]

MISCHIEF MAKERS

Janet Darby was the Chailey radiographer for almost 30 years, and her work in developing medical photography led to her also becoming the unofficial photographer of all the Heritage social events:

'I always remember my first week at Chailey in 1972. Unlike the cramped basement departments in hospitals, where I had worked previously, the X-ray department at Chailey was in a converted barn with what felt like acres of space, masses of natural light and the most beautiful views over open countryside to Ashdown Forest in the distance.

'After a chat with the radiographer I replaced, who had left at the end of the previous week, I got everything ready and rang up for three children to be sent over from the school by special transport. By normal standards this would have been a perfectly reasonable number, and in my innocent mid-twenties, with little experience of working with disabled children, I expected these three to be quiet, well-behaved and easy to X-ray. That was to be my first mistake of many.

'They arrived, and I took the first child into my new domain. Of course it took four times as long as I had expected, and when I opened the door into the little waiting room there were two wickedly grinning faces waiting for me, and the sound of the loo cistern refilling. They then told me, amid many giggles, that they had locked the outside door and flushed the key away. What can you do?

'I eventually got them to admit that they had simply thrown the key out of the window and, not wishing to lose too much face, I climbed out of the window, retrieved the key and proceded to X-ray the next child amid gales of laughter. After this baptism I never looked back.'

'I shall never forget the first time Dr Quibell gave his consent for us to go to Brighton for the day – the first time Princess Elizabeth Clinic had ever visited the sea.

'There was a helper for each child, and we went in the sea, had a picnic on the beach and walked down Brighton seafront eating ice creams and ignoring the comments made by passers-by. That was a wonderful day.'

'The children with gas-powered limbs were taken out shopping in Haywards Heath, and there was often some consternation among the public when the limbs began hissing – they made a frightful noise!'

was like with the Victorian era and its freak shows, then the Heritage in the 60s and 70s was like the Hilton. Compared with today, though, it was very bad. As young children you didn't get out very much in public because people didn't want to see you. Parents covered their children up with long jackets – that kind of thing. When we got to about 11 years old we were at least taken to a Saturday matinée club at Haywards Heath and sometimes to a youth club, too.'

Against this, it should perhaps be stressed that the staff, although conscious of public attitudes, did make strenuous efforts to take children out into the community virtually every week in order to get them accustomed to the outside world. Parents were encouraged to take their children home during the holidays, too, although some felt unable to cope with the pressures brought about by the physical disabilities and their social context. And inside?

At the experimental workshop and training centre opened by Princess Margaret in November 1963, and then known as the Lady Hoare Workshops, a team headed by Nigel Ring was to focus on the best way of using light-weight carbon fibre harnesses to support the weight of the gas-powered artifical arms fitted to the truncated upper limbs that some of the

Halfway through a hard-fought meal the gas would run out. The children were clever with them – one could even pick a daisy with his hook – but their feet were much more useful.

'Most of them had residual arms and feet or fingers, and they much preferred to use these.'

children were born with. Because these lightweight harnesses were accurately fitted to each child's body shape, the sense of the weight of the artificial arms was reduced – much as a well fitting rucksack feels lighter than a poorly fitting one which shifts about.

Ingeniously, 'proprioception' was built into the controls of the artificial arms which the children operated with their chins or with the vestiges of fingers they may have had. Children had an idea of where a limb was in space without having to look at it, much like a normal arm: as they moved a finger in one direction, so the arm would follow. There was also 'force feedback', in that the controls became heavier as the arm carried a greater weight. But the gas cylinders were cumbersome and had to be changed every two hours. One nurse remembered that the artifical arms spent a lot of time stuffed down the backs of radiators.

'They absolutely hated them,' says Verena Hanbury, 'because they felt that not only could they get around far better and more quickly on their seats on the floor in ways that they'd devised for themselves, but they had to carry a gas cylinder on their backs to power these limbs, and they really felt, I think, that they looked quite freaky. It wasn't worth the hassle, and so they really didn't want to wear them.

'They were some of the people I first got to know there, and even today some of them come back without their limbs and they're just themselves, and they get on better that way. An awful lot of work and research was put into these powered limbs, which really weren't a great success.'

Physiotherapist Joan Harben supervising play – quite hard work with the artificial limbs. [Nursing Times]

Louise, who went on to marry and have two children, has phocomelia (which means that she has 'flipper limbs'), and she suffered the stresses of the gas-powered substitutes. She and her friends often dispensed with them, to the consternation of staff – not surprising when you learn that the legs weighed a stone each and that the children moved around rather as if they were wearing stilts.

'They used a mixture of gas and water, and it was easy to mess about with the valves. There was a screw with a slot in the middle, and you could take a pencil or a ruler to it. The arms shot everywhere when you did that!'

Many of the teachers had doubts about the artificial limbs from the first. Eleanor Manvell taught 4–7-year-olds from 1964 until 1981, and she has vivid memories of the children arriving with the equipment on.

'They were so tedious for the children. I used to say "Would you give a little child sugar tongs to play with bricks?" That's

Nigel Ring and friend get to grips with a problem.

Editorial in Heritage News, autumn 1979: 'It is a sobering thought that very soon the last of the much loved Thalidomide children will have gone on from Chailey, and we wish them well in the far from easy world in which they will find themselves.'

what it was like. I felt that these little ones needed to use whatever they had of their own, even if it was just a tiny hand on the end of a shoulder.

'There were some dreadful falls because of the legs. They called them rockers, because the only way to move was by rocking from side to side. They wore helmets, but there will still some nasty accidents. The children would ask me: "Can I have my legs off?" They hated them.

'I must say, though, that the physios were very good about it – as the occupational therapists were. We came to a compromise. The children would be allowed to play on the floor without their artificial limbs, but there were some activities which required them. When they wanted to paint, for example, they needed their legs in order to be able to stand. They understood that, and so they wore them for part of the day.'

In about 1975 powered limbs were at last abandoned, but Nigel Ring (interviewed in the winter 1981 issue of *Heritage News*) regarded it as 'wise after the event' to suggest that the effort had been mistaken.

'How could anyone tell, when they were as small as that, that they would develop such incredible resilience and ingenuity in adapting to life? At the time, both clinically and scientifically, let alone compassionately, I am sure it was the right decision to develop powered artificial limbs. They failed by and large for a number of reasons. On the one hand the children developed so quickly that they were always ahead of us in their demands. But on the other it was the technical shortcomings which floored us – the appalling weight of the apparatus, the cylinders of compressed carbon dioxide always running out, and the inability to communicate *feeling* through powered limbs.'

The work had not been wasted, however. The Heritage, with generous support from the Department of Health, was now recognised as being in the forefront of so-called rehabilitation engineering.

Rehabilitation

*I*t was Philip Quibell who set Chailey on the road to worldwide renown in the field of rehabilitation, the work of the Lady Hoare Experimental Workshop developing naturally from what he had started before. He had become interested in the subject while working at Treloar Hospital before the war, and he quickly set about building up the therapeutic team at the Heritage: occupational therapy, for instance, was introduced in the person of Jill Rockey, who arrived in 1952 and strengthened the physiotherapy department.

Long before the workshop was established, John Florence had been visiting the Heritage to fit children with splints. His son (also John), would eventually set up his Orthotic Workshop in two portakabins at the New Heritage in 1975 – claiming to be the first privately owned workshop in the country to operate from hospital premises.

'Orthotics,' explained an article in the spring 1976 issue of *Heritage News*, 'is the splinting of any disabled part of the body, and Mr Florence and his team of workers make all the apparatus the children at Chailey wear.'

A leading instigator in the setting up of the experimental workshop was Ian Fletcher, a doctor at Roehampton Hospital, where the early artificial limbs had previously been made. He and his team are remembered for being relaxed with the children and encouraging them to express their views about the equipment they were the very first to wear.

Jill Sharpe, writing on 'My apparatus' in the 1965 school magazine:
'I have two chairs and two sets of gadgets to fix on to them. One set is to help me to write and it consists of two metal bars to fix to the chair, an arm rest with a clip to fix a pen in, and a spare one in case it breaks. The other set is to help me to eat, and it also consists of two metal bars and an arm rest, but also a spoon which is half a spoon and half a fork – its original name being a spork. I have also two rings to put round the plate to stop the food coming off. For my typing I have two gadgets called distaffs, which are fairly long poles with "dobers" on the end. They are operated by the feet, and I enjoy using them.'

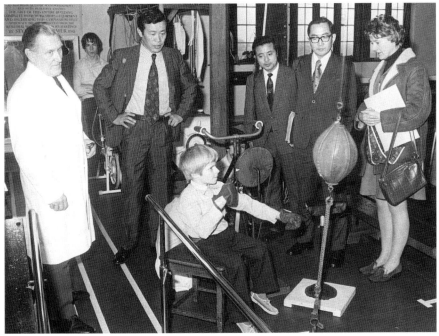

International recognition: Japanese visitors in 1976 watch Stephen Simmons using a punchbag to strengthen his limbs. On the left is Eric Diagre, the remedial gymnast, while Dr Gillian McCarthy can be seen on the right.

John Florence eventually had a staff of eight (supplying not only Chailey, but most of the London hospitals, too), although he was the only one actually to deal with the Heritage children – measuring, fitting, designing and assembling all the apparatus. He worked closely with doctors and therapists to produce equipment which was user-friendly and acceptable to the children, and he was proud of the fact that the workshop could usually put a piece of apparatus together in a week, whereas his nearest rivals took three months.

Nigel Ring was appointed technical director of the rehabilitation engineering unit in 1967, when it was set up to research work on artificial limbs for children damaged by Thalidomide. A Cambridge graduate in mechanical engineering, he had joined the Heritage in 1966, three years after the Lady Hoare workshops had been established with a staff of just two technicians and an occupational therapist. His speciality had been the study of powered artificial limbs, but his unit continued to grow rapidly despite the eventual failure of that experiment. In 1972, for instance, new money was found both for research and to extend the building, with new members of staff appointed, too.

Hilary Ford, who worked at the Heritage from 1965 until 1989, remembers with gratitude the efforts of the rehabilitation engineering unit.

'We were fortunate to have the workshop almost on top of us, and they produced perfectly adapted spoons and every other utensil available. Each

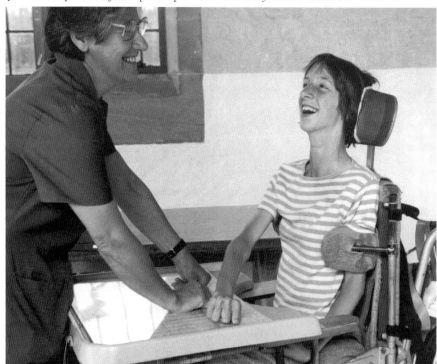

Ruth Cartwright and Ruth McCormack enjoying themselves in physio. The two left Chailey at the same time in 1989, the former after 31 years of service and the latter at the age of 17. [Janet Darby]

child was different, and so the work was very time-consuming. Washing, cleaning teeth, dressing, toileting, eating and school work all had to be experimented with. Loops on clothes for adjusting with a finger or toe. Velcro to do things up (Velcro was not widely used then). Spoons for use with feet or one finger. Pencil and paint brush holders for the mouth, to be steadied by a finger.

'At this stage the children went out in baby buggies, and so we had lots of double baby buggies to cut the staff ratio. The children with spina bifida also had problems. They were very prone to sores, so we had to have every hard surface they used covered with PVC foam. Their legs broke easily, too, and they therefore had to be treated with care.'

One of the fields of research was alternative seating for children with spina bifida and cerebral palsy, and this became the speciality of Roy Nelham – appointed as a research engineer in 1973 and technical director (Rehabilitation Engineering) from 1981 until he retired in 2002.

'Many of the children need support for their spines and for weak muscles,' he explains. 'Unless you're sitting properly you get sores, and you're inefficient in sitting up in the classroom. Plywood and foam were effective but costly, and they were hard to fit accurately. We developed moulded plastic seating, and we designed and produced a vacuum-forming machine.'

In 1978 he was awarded a Churchill travelling fellowship to visit Canada and America for four weeks. The American government had already set up ten so-called 'rehabilitation engineering' centres, and that title was adopted by the Chailey unit later that year. Roy Nelham subsequently wrote a report on what he had discovered, but *Heritage News* readers were given a preview in the summer issue that year.

'There are two main research projects related to seating,' he wrote. 'In Winnipeg, lines are projected onto the patient's body to produce a contour map which is analysed by computer. The resulting information would be transmitted to a machine on which it is possible to cut the patient's shape out of solid foam to make a seat. This project has only just begun and no results are yet available.

'The other main research project is making use of thermography, which is a technique for measuring temperatures by using a camera similar to a television camera. This is a known procedure for screening for breast cancer, and is being used to measure the temperature effects caused by different types of seat. After the patient has been sitting on a cushion for about 30 minutes, his skin is exposed

Roy Nelham

Pete Tutt, manager of the Rehabilitation Engineering workshop today, with one of the trikes made for the children at Chailey. [James Luscombe]

Current research and innovation areas at Chailey include sleep (Dr Yasmin Khan, one of the consultants, is an honorary senior lecturer at Great Ormond Street); the use of treatments in movement disorders; long-term follow-up for hip dislocation; treatment for drooling, includIng palatal training therapy; users' experiences of postural management equipment; an assessment tool for powered mobility users; psychiatric indicators for children after brain injury; and a follow-up study after spinal fusion.

The special seats and lying and standing supports designed and developed as part of Chailey's '24-hour approach to postural management' have been widely acclaimed and imitated. They are now available nationwide, and work is under way in New Zealand to replicate the equipment there.

and the thermographic camera used to study the temperature changes taking place on the buttocks. In this way the effectiveness of various cushions can be assessed and cushion designs changed accordingly.

'At each centre visited I gave a talk about our work at Chailey, and there was a general free exchange of information. Quite a lot of the information I collected can be put to good use here at Chailey or elsewhere in the UK, and the contacts that I made will enable me to continue the information exchange into the future.'

The unit was renamed the Rehabilitation Engineering Service (RES) when it moved to the Westfield site, and Roy Nelham is justly proud of what it has achieved.

'Most of the technology mentioned in this book has emanated from it,' he says, 'and in this way the RES contributes significantly to the difference that Chailey Heritage can make to disabled children and their families and carers. Individual assessment and problem-solving processes for the many problems experienced by the children enables the REU staff – working closely with therapists – to apply, adapt or invent an appropriate piece of equipment, now referred to as assistive technology or assistive devices.'

A display by the wheelchair dancing team, c. 1976.

It's a far cry from the days when the Heritage carpenter Tom Milham, ('a lovely, gentle man who finished his work lovingly,' remembers one of the nurses who worked alongside him), made wheeled trolleys on which boys out of their calipers used to scoot around the dormitories at St George's.

Research on seating was most recently developed by Elizabeth Green who, starting work at the Heritage in 1981, joined the seating clinic team. During the 1980s she not only undertook a psychology degree but also completed a doctorate based on the effect of different seating systems on the performance, including psychological, of physically handicapped children. This work, along with a great many other Chailey initiatives, has won international recognition.

'I'd worked at a special school with children with more severe disability than those at Chailey at that time,' she says, 'Some of them had horrific spinal curvatures, with their ribs rubbing against their pelvic bones. They hadn't been born like that, but life with gravity and growth had combined to cause the damage. I thought that something could be done to prevent this.

'A major task we set ourselves was to find ways of reducing deformity. It's very easy for children with severe neurological problems to lose the skills they do have, so that, for example, they become unable to use their hands. With two research therapists, Catey Mulcahy and Terry Pountney, I undertook a study which looked at 'normal' babies and the way and rate at which they develop to discover how we could apply that knowledge to our care at Chailey. We came up with the "Chailey Levels of Ability".

'One of our early projects, with funding from the Department of Health,' says Dr Green, 'was designing a seating system that went into a wheelchair. We later had a four-year research grant from Action Research and devised the "Chailey Approach to Postural Management", designing a teaching package which is used nationally.

'Research had been going at the Heritage for some years before this, particularly into the design of moulded seating, a "Chailey Chariot" and a moulded toilet seat. The latter is made by a manufacturer but remains widely known as "the Chailey toilet seat". Other research studies with funding from the Department of Health and the Spastics Society were completed, linked with measurement of posture and the use of electronic switches for computer and powered wheelchair access.'

In 1975 Nigel Ring, always aware of new technological developments, had appointed Andrew Brown to run an electronic department in the unit. Previously, he said, problems which clearly could best be solved electronically had had to 'submit to mechanical solutions' because the staff had a greater knowledge in that area.

'Micro-electronics – the silicon chip – is going to have the greatest impact for the handicapped,' he said, 'particularly in improving their ability to communicate, where this is impaired, and in their education, employment and leisure activities.'

The latest version of the Chailey toilet seat.

'The children learned to point to their Bliss boards with switches driven by their head, chin or shoulders. So on the whole the wheelchair driving was worked out first and then, if satisfactory, adapted for a computer when needed. This meant that all the children had to have their own computers.

'If their spasms were not under control they could do very little, so they needed a good seat with a lapstrap. The feet were firmly planted on the foot rests, and tied there if necessary, to help the sitting position. Any part of the body which a child could control would be used.

'All of this equipment had to go backwards and forwards for weekends and holidays, from Chailey to home. A small car was useless!'

Heritage News, autumn 1979: 'The Grand Old Man himself [Charles Bliss], who is now 82, visited Chailey earlier this year from his home in Toronto where he has established a centre for the study of communication problems in cerebral palsy and other sufferers from multiple verbal handicaps.

'Having suffered the hardships of concentration camps and seen at close hand man's inhumanity to man, he conceived the idea of creating a universal symbol language to break down the barriers of misunderstanding between nations, and it was only comparatively recently that its marvellous potential for the physically handicapped has been realised.'

Back in 1962 the head of IBM's design department had presented the Heritage with (the school magazine reported) 'two very expensive electric typewriters'. These presumably replaced the second-hand model which Jill Rockey (occupational therapist at Chailey and for Brighton Health District from 1952–1985) remembers very clearly. This was the up-to-the-minute communication tool in those days.

'We of course had to adapt the typewriter for the children,' she says. 'We used nuts and bolts, plastic and knicker elastic!'

Communications has long been a major area for research.

'The plight of athetoid children,' Nigel Ring had admitted in 1975, 'is, to some extent, one of the most unsatisfactory of any at the Heritage. The frustrating combination of negligible speech and poorly co-ordinated limb movements makes communication very difficult. In order to try to make some small in-road into their problem we are currently applying for a grant to make a two-year appointment of an experimental psychologist to carry out some exploratory work.'

Chailey had by then begun to develop the system devised by Charles Bliss, who established a centre for the study of communication problems in cerebral palsy and other sufferers from multiple verbal handicaps. The 'Blissymbols' are single-line drawings which depict common thoughts and ideas. Their use was developed by Carol Walker, and their advantages (sometimes double-edged) were explained by Nigel Ring at the time.

A Blissful welcome to the Queen Mother from Patricia Brown on her 1983 visit. [Janet Darby]

'Blissymbols are drawn on a chart which the child points to with his finger, a head-stick, or, as in the case of many Chailey children, with his eyes, using a code. The word is always written under the symbol so that a child can talk to the "uninitiated". Also, Blissymbols are fun! With them children can become creative, making up stories and jokes. They can also be cheeky or rude. I was embarrassed recently when I introduced two visitors to a child using Blissymbols who promptly showed that he didn't want to be interrupted by telling my

High tech, 1976 style. The caption in a Heritage scrapbook reads: 'David Levett shows how his Talking Brooch lets people know what he wants to say. His classmates bought it with a sponsored swim.'

The Chailey Communication System (CCS) was officially launched in March 1996 by the actor Bob Hoskins.

Students are today encouraged to use a 'total approach', both developing their own excellent non-verbal skills and using a range of other systems, including so-called voice output communication aids (VOCAs).

Staff and pupils are currently using Signalong, which provides a basic vocabulary of 1600 signs based on British Sign Language, as well as a variety of different symbols and word systems to meet each individual's needs.

colleagues to "get lost". Fortunately this did not offend them, but converted them, since they became convinced it allowed the child to say what he wanted.'

Heather Couper, teaching at the school from the late 60s, has a similar memory regarding the first computer introduced to the Heritage shortly before she retired in 1987.

'We played noughts and crosses on it, and I shall never forget how lovely it was to see one little boy laugh like anything when he found he was able to cheat!'

A later intake of children with greater learning disabilities would struggle with the abstract set of symbols used by Bliss, and the Heritage later introduced the Makaton system.

Electronics have since opened up the kind of possibilities Nigel Ring hardly dared dream of. Only a few years ago, most children in wheelchairs had to be pushed everywhere, relying upon the choices of their carers: the children might indicate a preference of route, but they had no means of following it for themselves. Take a walk around the Heritage today, inside or out, and you'll see children making their own decisions about where to go. They're using the track and SCAD (sonic collision avoidance device) systems invented by the school's electronics engineer Martin Langer, who has been at the Heritage for some 20 years and has spent more than a decade developing ever more sophisticated mobility devices.

Above: Tony Bown makes a repair to a Chailey posture seat in the Rehabilitation Engineering workshop. His son Louis is a pupil in the primary department at the Heritage. [James Luscombe]
Below: Tyler Russell sets the bear blowing bubbles in the adventure corridor. [James Luscombe]
Facing page: Inside St Martin's chapel. [Alistair Bruce]

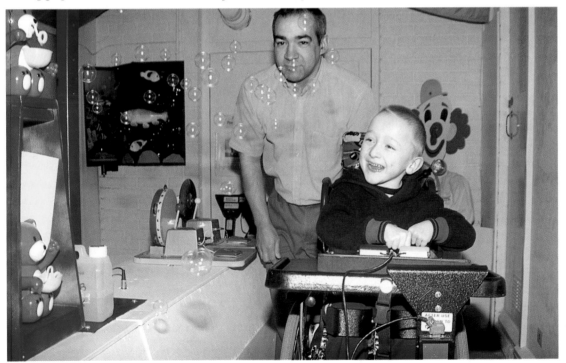

'The best thing about having a barn-like ward was space. When children were learning to drive their powered wheelchairs through doors and round furniture and out into the garden, it was invaluable. Remember, these children had never crawled, and so had never learned "space". They had to learn it in an electric wheelchair – quite a challenge to the walls and doors, I can tell you!'

One result is an increase in sheer fun. The school's 'adventure corridor' (*see page 131*) allows children to take themselves through a colourful tunnel, activating controls which make bells ring, music play, gusts of air blow hot or cold, a fish wag its tail, a bear blow bubbles, a clown inflate a balloon . . . This is a kind of sensory experience which would have been impossible in the past.

The chief purpose of this advanced technology, however, is to give the children greater independence. The track system – which was established some years ago and runs all round the school – allows them to follow metal strips in the floor, deciding at junctions whether to turn right or left: a miniature wire carrying a very low voltage current is buried under floor coverings. SCAD, more sophisticated, has 'electronic eye' sensors built in to wheelchairs (developed from the automatic focusing technology used in cameras), and this keeps them away from walls and oncoming 'vehicles', the children being otherwise able to turn in any direction they wish.

'In the past,' explains Martin Langer, 'staff have necessarily made a great many decisions affecting mobility, but now we're giving the children a greater choice. It's a challenging area. We're trying to keep the systems as simple as possible. Too much clever technology gets in the way of the learning process – after all, if everything is built into the wheelchair a child won't learn as much about coping with the physical world as if he or she were crashing it into the walls! We also have to be aware of fatigue levels, and we're giving the children the opportunity of switching from SCAD system to the track system when they grow tired.'

The new, excitingly empowering technology, has made its mark in the IT field, too. The children can now manouevre their wheelchairs to dock with their computer stations and 'log on' themselves.

Meanwhile, Martin Langer entered the centenary year working on perhaps the most exciting project to date. The idea is to create a network of 'audio signposts' all over the school, with the children picking up messages on loudspeaker units built into their chairs as they drive around.

'The approach of a wheelchair to one of the beacons we install will tell the children where they are, and we'll be able to personalise the information, too. So a voice might say "Hello, Tommy, you're just approaching the chapel" – and it could even be the voice of Tommy's mother!

'For the children it will be an invaluable enhancement of the school environment.'

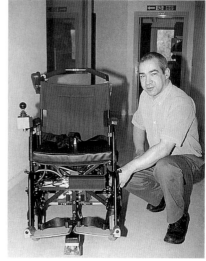

Martin Langer demonstrates a chair fitted with the SCAD system.

HERITAGE NEWS

The first issue of Heritage News was published in September 1969. The idea had come from Reg Bullock, the hospital secretary (tragically killed in a car accident a month later), and its aim was to provide up-to-date news of what was going on at Chailey for voluntary workers, who contributed so much to the welfare of the children, and for staff working at the Heritage's scattered locations – the Old Heritage, the New Heritage and St George's.

A few years later the children themselves began to read it, and then the parents. It became a magazine written for, and by, anyone involved with the Heritage: children, staff, voluntary helpers, old scholars, parents and the League of Friends.

It originally appeared three times a year, and it was published without a break until spring 1996. The first editor was Angela Wigglesworth, a local freelance journalist and a 'substitute parent' at the Heritage. After six years she passed it on to another local journalist, Kim Protheroe, who was to be followed by Colin Davis, the editor for many years.

The cover photograph for the very first issue of Heritage News, showing the carousel made for the children by prisoners at Lewes gaol. They invited about 30 children to a party at the prison, gave them rides on the carousel and entertained them with comedy sketches. [Tony Tree/Angela Wigglesworth]

From an article by speech therapist Jenny Barrett in the first edition of Heritage News: 'Having arranged my timetable, the next and greater problem was to find my children. Inevitably they have changed classrooms, gone to the clinic, gone to the dentist, "run out of gas", are sick with the flu.

'It is unfortunate and maybe peculiar to Chailey, that many wards and other buildings have alternative names. To the newcomer it is very confusing: for example, to be told that your child is on "Big End", not "Little End", or in "Waterloo" for a clinic.

'The children knew me before I knew most of them. They soon had me classified as "the speech lady", and inevitably all wanted to come and see me. Because they are resident they all love to have that individual attention.'

Facing page (top and bottom): Barty Graham and Laura Sommerford enjoying a music session. Music plays a big part in Chailey Heritage's multi-sensory approach to the curriculum.

Right: Ross Gill in the saddle at the new all-weather riding surface, officially opened in the Heritage's centenary year.

Below: The new swimming pool, opened by footballer Gary Lineker in 1997, is a vital aid for physiotherapy. The mural was painted by Dame Grace's great granddaughter Robyn Horsburgh.

[James Luscombe]

THE HERITAGE FESTIVAL

The Heritage Festival was held in September 1972, raising some £800 for improvements to the 59-year-old chapel organ. There were concerts, a flower show in the chapel, an art exhibition in the school, a disco and barbecue, cheese and wine parties and a dispay of old photographs and documents.

Mirror Grange, the dolls' house made for Daily Mirror characters Pip, Squeak and Wilfred was restored for the festival by inmates of Lewes Prison who, in their spare time, had volunteered to repair and refurbish it after it had been in storage for some 40 years.

Each night at the Old Heritage there was a son et lumiere performance which told the story of the Heritage. Apples were hung on the tree outside the chapel to remind visitors of Dame Grace Kimmins' 1930s campaign which had raised a large sum to build St George's on the common.

The golden apple tree fruits again. [*photo-technique/* Angela Wigglesworth]

The Great Reorganisation

'Chailey Heritage? That's closing down, isn't it?' Rumours such as this during the run-up period to the reorganisation of the National Health Service in 1974 led to a staff meeting in the autumn of 1973 at which Philip Quibell spoke defiantly about the future of Chailey.

'The time has come to let people know where we stand,' he said. 'The size of the Heritage will not alter. There is a move in the country to get disabled people looked after locally, but these services are at present inadequate. A place like the Heritage will go on for a long time because other services are not available.'

These were brave words, but Dr Quibell was surely speaking more in hope than expectation. The truth was that the very future of Chailey hung in the balance. From the spring of 1972 there had been a series of official visits and reports undertaken by the hospital advisory service of the NHS, expressing the view that although the Heritage provided an outstanding service for children with severe physical handicap, it was 'much less successful in helping the children to overcome the loss of a home and family'.

The advisory service was particularly uneasy about the under-7s, whom it felt should not be living in a formal hospital setting, and some children who had been admitted to Chailey 'primarily because of a failure in provision elsewhere rather than because of the unique services of Chailey'. There was a need, it said, to review the extent to which the hospital should continue to provide a national service.

In a detailed evaluation of Chailey's history, the report acknowledged that residential care in the country had initially been regarded as a humane regime for handicapped children. It conceded, too, that the Heritage was well run, but it found that only the emphasis on schooling differentiated the patient's day from that experienced in short-stay children's hospitals.

Again, although the quality of nursing was excellent, 'the "hospital" attitudes and traditional organisation of nursing time and roles leads to a less satisfactory conclusion regarding the social and emotional well-being of patients when many may be disturbed by their abnormalities and deprived of a normal home life.' There was a danger of the hospital 'passively acting as a "refuge" for deformed and crippled children'.

Perhaps the most significant aspects of the report concerned patient welfare and social service provisions. The visiting team noted that the Heritage was 'isolated in heathland', making it difficult for children to have a normal experience of life – 'the local school, the street where they live, travelling on buses and going to the local libraries and coffee bars'.

Although team planning was good, the report continued, the first duty of the assessment team should be to decide whether a child needed hospitalisation in the first place. Recommendations were made with regard to individual parts of the Heritage, including the urgent need to divide the junior dormitory into two or three family-sized units and the need to restore children under the age of four to their families or to an appropriate child care organisation.

How would Grace Kimmins have responded to the reorganisation?

'She would have summoned the chairman of the Area Health Authority to Chailey,' Verena Hanbury suggested in an address in the chapel on Old Scholars' Day. 'She would have thanked him endlessly for the time and trouble he was taking planning our future. She would then have begged a few moments of his attention while she told him what the future was actually going to be and then, as she showed him out, she would have allowed him the honour of signing a cheque towards her latest appeal.'

Instead, Verena Hanbury invited area adminstrator Gilbert Bourne to the Nativity play.

'To our joy he came, and I think it is fair to say he got the message.'

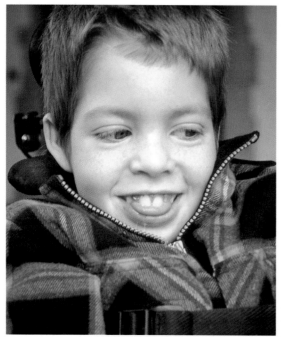
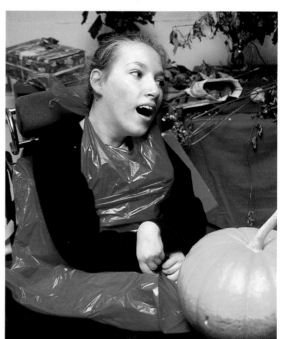

Top left: Tomas Cremades-Hashemi.
Top right: Danielle Lees preparing a pumpkin lantern.
Above: Timmy Henry hard at work on a PC.
[James Luscombe]

Top: John Giles working on one-to-one counting.
Above: Amy Saunders working in a craft session.
[James Luscombe]

Not all of these ideas were anathema to Heritage staff, since they reflected a prevailing shift in emphasis from institutional to family care and from a 'hospital model' to an educational one. There were, however, fears and disagreements. The headmaster, Harry Browning, rejected the argument that children of nursery school age should not remain at the Heritage for longer periods.

'This is directly against the current educational thought,' he said, 'which has long been saying that it is desperately important to have good nursery school provision for handicapped children. Unless we have a good basis in nursery school, other teachers have nothing on which to build.

'We are determined not to have children at the Heritage who are severely sub-normal without being physically handicapped. If they dash about without sufficient intelligence to tell them what is good or bad they could be a serious danger to the more delicate of the handicapped children.'

The Chailey house committee agreed with the advisory service's wish to return the children to their families, but felt that 'in practice the lack of alternatives appears to override it'. While treatment in some local hospitals might be possible, 'there are cases where the "total care" concept requires admission to a long-stay unit with comprehensive facilities'.

At this sensitive moment in the debate a letter was sent from the Department of Health and Social Security to the South East Metropolitan Regional Board. It was 'disturbing', it declared, 'that one of the foremost hospitals providing long-term accommodation for physically handicapped children is not providing total care'.

Mark Barnett shows his cooking prowess.
[*Doug McKenzie*]

It considered what it deemed to be 'unnecessary admissions', and asked what could be done to stop them within a reasonably short time – 'say eighteen months'. It also enquired about the scope for moving existing patients in this category to more appropriate accommodation near their homes. Chailey, it urged, should cease to provide a national service and, within the region itself, it should be replaced by small local units.

An advisory team sent by the Board to the Heritage in October 1972 accepted its general conclusions. The low bed occupancy and limited waiting list suggested that there should be a gradual reduction in the size of the Heritage. Major surgery should be carried out elsewhere, saving £80,000 on theatre facilities, and visiting consultants should, as they retired, be replaced by staff from hospitals in Brighton.

Within weeks of Dr Quibell's bold pronouncement, the school governors and the hospital house committee were rocked on their heels by another explosive letter – this one from the newly-formed South East Thames Regional Health Authority. From April 1974 this authority would control a number of area health authorities, within which there would be several health districts (the Heritage being under Brighton district and the East Sussex area). This letter stated that the number of beds at the Heritage should be between 120 and 150 – Dr Quibell had argued that 'the size must remain not less than 200 children to retain the number and range of staff' – and reported the concern of the regional health board 'that *if Chailey were to remain in existence* [author's italics] it should have a definite and worthwhile function in order to sustain staff morale and the present valuable local support.'

Further proposals outlined in this letter were that no children under 3–4 should be admitted for long periods; that children from long distances should not be long-stay patients; and that facilities should be developed for the on-going care of those physically handicapped patients who could not be absorbed into the community, with provision made for these patients to stay on beyond the age of 16.

This last suggestion was eagerly taken up by the Heritage, but the huge uncertainties about its very existence still weighed heavily upon it. A conference of chief and assistant education officers of Brighton, Eastbourne and the two counties of East and West Sussex was called at Chailey in January 1974.

'The education officers were unanimous,' read the subsequent minutes of this meeting, 'that Chailey Heritage is the major centre of physically handicapped children in this area and should continue as such. LEAs should get together to preserve the school. Places for ambulant children vacated because of hospital decisions to reduce beds should be filled by children who do not need hospital treatment so as to help maintain the present size of the school.

'It was, however, important not to lose the valuable hospital contact. If a non-maintained special school were to be established at Chailey Heritage in lieu of the present hospital school, the cost of the pupils' boarding as well as tuition would fall on LEAs; viz. an increase from the present £552 per annum (tuition) to approximately £1300 per annum (tuition and boarding).'

It was backs-to-the-wall time.

Sister Verity Hines in Heritage News: 'One boy the other day asked me something about when I was a child and wore calipers. I had to tell him I never did wear them.

'Up to their arrival here, I think they feel they will grow out of their handicaps, but when they see the 16-year-olds on the same ward they must realise they don't. I think perhaps this idea has grown up because they see very few disabled adults.'

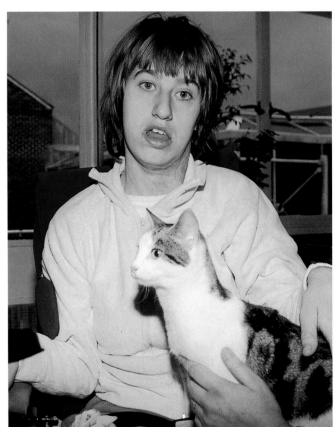

Left: Dona Bignell on pet day. Staff and pupils brought in their pets to allow fellow pupils to experience different animal behaviours, movements and coat/skin textures.

Below: William Thomas in Pre-School.

Facing page, above: Graham Barber, with some of the products of the Enterprise Centre.

Facing page, below: A colourful bug at Westfield, the Chailey base of the South Downs NHS Trust. All the medical, therapy and rehabilitation engineering services are under one roof, including outpatient clinic rooms and a radiology department. There is also a seminar room and reference library for the staff.

[James Luscombe]

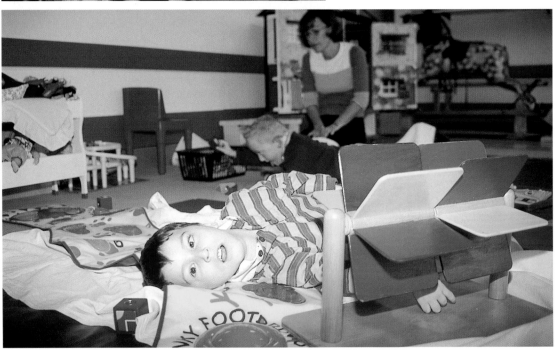

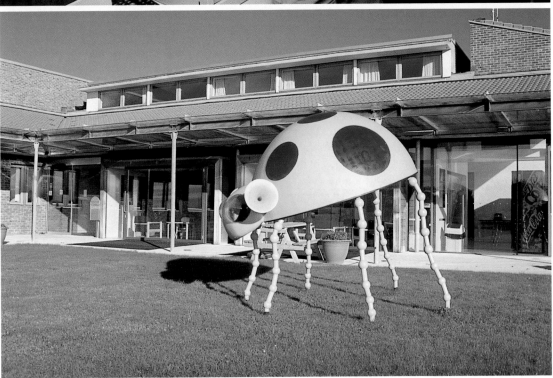

The Warren Connection

Michael Warren during the 1970s.

The disbanding of the house committee in 1974 brought an end to the close involvement of three generations of the Warren family in the development of the Heritage.

Mrs T.P. Warren was among the invaluable band of supporters in the very early days of Grace Kimmins' ambitious colony in Sussex. Her son, Col. J.R. (Raymond) Warren, similarly gave both time and considerable money to the cause, creating the nurses' home which bore the family name and the marine annexe at Tidemills. Michael Warren and his wife, Gillian, followed the example set by his parents: she was active in the Friends, while Mr Warren joined the house committee in 1965 and was elected chairman in 1972.

Among his earliest memories of the Heritage are occasions during which, as a very young boy, it was his task to present a purse full of money to a visiting member of the royal family – 'a silk purse with gold strings, as I recall.' A more alarming experience was the day on which his father was unable to take the salute at a Heritage march-past ('there was a military air to Chailey then, and the whole jolly place marched by in proper military order'), leaving the young Michael to stand to attention while everyone performed the eyes-right procedure in his direction: 'My father should have been there, but he'd sent this wretched little lad along in his place!'

A fund of good stories, Mr Warren tells of the day when the Daily Express came to research a feature on the Heritage, Mrs Kimmins having overlooked the fact that this was a visiting day by the Harley Street surgeons who regularly gave their time and skills to the children free of charge.

'You can imagine the deep pleasure of the consultants,' he laughs 'arriving in their Rolls Royces and entering the wards to discover photographers flashing away, asking the children to turn their heads in this and that direction. Mrs Kimmins had to pour a lot of oil on troubled waters after that – which of course she was very good at doing.'

While he was chairman of the house committe, Mr Warren and Verena Hanbury decided to mount a fire drill, using dramatic smoke bombs.

'We put one in a dustbin at St George's and tried to merge unseen into the background while huge plumes of dirty-coloured smoke billowed into the stairwell. The amazing thing is that life went on completely as normal. The occasional nurse went by and asked what it was all about. The odd job man growled that it was a terrible mess that he'd have to clear up later. We stood there with a stop watch, wondering how long it would be before anyone took any action. Minutes went by. Eventually people broke into a slow trot and dealt with it, but a real fire would have been disastrous. The fire service were extraordinarily charitable about it, but I can tell you that quite a few lessons were learned that day!'

New Brooms

*I*n the spring of 1983 readers opened Chailey's house magazine, *Heritage News*, to read an astonishing paragraph written by its editor, Colin Davis.

'Once it ceased to have a whole time medical director,' it ran, 'and Big Brother disbanded the totally dedicated house committee, Chailey inevitably became a remote control, departmentalised, NHS institution in which the right hand knew not what the left was doing. Only a few vestigial remains of the old order, like the Nativity Play, are left to remind us of a now legendary past. Many of the buildings which made up the "public school of crippledom" (how archaic that title now sounds) are no longer what our present administrators would term economically viable, and the splendid chapel is no longer central to the life of the Heritage.'

These provocative opinions, which might have been written by Dame Grace's ghost in a dyspeptic mood, created a storm – and an immediate riposte from Chailey's two consultants. In the next issue of the magazine the consultant paediatric neurologist, Richard Robinson, flatly told Mr Davis that he was mistaken in his 'remote control' comment.

'Chailey,' he said, 'is run on the principle of consensus, and this is embodied in the professional advisory committee on which there are representatives not only of all the departments at Chailey but also of the Brighton District, who are extremely sympathetic to our needs and who can handle the very difficult problems of modern administrations which would be beyond our capabilities.

'We find that in working together a right decision usually crystallises and that a "leader" is rarely necessary.'

A more detailed retaliation was delivered by way of a letter from Gillian McCarthy, Chailey's consultant paediatrician, which claimed that 'many people, particularly among the present staff at Chailey, found the editorial inaccurate and outdated in its views'.

Dr McCarthy had arrived in 1975, shortly after the seismic shake-up in the health service. She had not only seen Chailey survive, but she had observed – and had instigated – many changes. These she now vigorously defended.

'The house committee had already been disbanded in 1974,' she wrote, 'and the professional advisory committee was in being, at that time very ably chaired by Nigel Ring. The present chairman is Richard Robinson. This committee consists of the heads of all departments of the hospital and school, and is involved in guiding and planning the work of Chailey. It makes recommendations on all areas of our work and the use of the endowment funds. The committee has been responsible for the production of annual reports on the work of Chailey which are considered a model for the rest of the Brighton Health District hospitals.

'The functioning of Chailey Heritage depends on decisions arrived at by consensus, and the medical directors (who are of course now two consultants) no longer fulfil the 'matriarchal' role. The links we have with

Hugh Parrott, on becoming headmaster in 1981:

'Being a disabled young person growing up today is as hard as it ever has been. I believe in giving guidance and offering a helping hand where it is needed, but the essence of any good relationship is mutual trust.

'Trust means respect, and respect must be worked for by children and adults alike. I also think that those things that come easily to us, however young we are, are most easily taken away. I don't see Chailey as my promised land, but I'm going to give it the love and respect it deserves.'

Richard Robinson, Heritage News, autumn 1983: 'Chailey is run on the principle of consensus. We find that in working together a right decision usually crystallises and that a "leader" is rarely necessary.'

Guy's Hospital via Dr Robinson and the Royal Alexandra Hospital in Brighton, where I also work, have increased our ability to help and treat the children.

'Other changes have occurred at Chailey in response to changing attitudes towards handicapped children and their families. So we have sought to keep children at home or closely linked with their families by weekly boarding wherever possible. The ability to change and adapt is a sign of vigour, not decadence, and does not indicate any lack of respect for the past. We value the traditions of Chailey and would see them continue. Surely one of the founder's traits was her ability to see what was required at that time, and she was ahead of her time in care of the handicapped.

'So we look forward to being able to set up a research project linked to the expertise of speech therapists, occupational therapists, physiotherapists and teachers to devise way to help children who cannot speak, by using electronic technology. Chailey has a unique mix of professionals dedicated to working as a team, and we believe that our future depends on our ability to develop the team approach.'

This was not only a devastating reply, but a striking in-a-nutshell picture of what had happened at Chailey in its new life after reorganisation. Dr McCarthy was to work at Chailey until 1998, and remains closely involved.

'The changes were essential,' she says today. 'I'd thought long and hard before applying for the consultant post, and I actually withdrew my first application after visiting the Heritage. I had been trained at forward-looking paediatric centres, namely Great Ormond Street, Northwick Park Hospital and Bristol Children's Hospital. At Chailey I was overwhelmed by the sight of so many children with severe physical disabilities in a hospital setting with no parents in evidence. I didn't even believe in boarding school!

'It was only after I was invited to think again that I realised that I might have very good qualifications for the job. Most of all I believed that the child should be seen as part of a family, and that the family should play a much greater role in the child's life. (I later learned the difficulties of achieving families for some of the children who had been at Chailey for most of their lives.)

'An institution can't replace a family. There was, I have to say, a great deal of resistance to the idea that anything was wrong with the system, but our aim was to make sure that families were much more closely involved.

Caught on camera in 1983 are Margaret Bruce, deputy head, with Tom Galletly, Chailey chaplain and warden at St George's. [Janet Darby]

'My predecessor's speciality had been orthopaedics, and he did an enormous amount in creating a multi-disciplinary team, and in the fields of assessment and rehabilitation. He had also introduced proper occupational and speech therapy and a good psychologist. But Chailey needed a paediatrician who worked here rather than simply visited. It had been very much an institution, a hospital. Many of the children had come as babies, and they'd spent their lives living in a hospital. Paediatricians didn't, and don't, think that way.'

Dr Gillian McCarthy

One innovation during the mid-1970s was the building of two bungalows on the New Heritage site, close to the rehabilitation unit. Reed Cottage was opened in May 1974, and it was so successful that Quibell Cottage (Philip Quibell had been the inspiration behind the project) followed soon afterwards. Both were funded by the League of Friends, and their purpose was to help prepare older children near the end of their time at Chailey for life in the outside world.

Two children would spend a weekend in the bungalows with an occupational therapist. They would shop, cook and practise all the other skills they would need when coping for themselves elsewhere. Physiotherapists would contribute to overcoming any difficulties encountered, and other members of staff would be encouraged to visit for tea, or simply for a chat.

Similarly, Leyden House at North Chailey and Walsingham House in Hove were locations where children who didn't go home at weekends or for holidays could be taken for a taste of more relaxed life outside the Heritage. Although there were a few paid staff at each, many Chailey staff were involved in a voluntary capacity, and there was also great input from an army of volunteers.

'In 1975 there were more than 200 children, nearly all resident,' says Gillian McCarthy. 'Now there are a hundred, and none lives there all the time. Children who are boarding go home at the weekend, while others come in for respite care. The children coming from other areas of the country we now see as outpatients. They're able to come for an appointment or to stay for up to a week with their family for assessment and advice in bungalows reserved for this purpose.

'In the past families couldn't face having children with severe limb deficiencies at home. Now we see children without limbs as outpatients, and we link them with adults with similar limb deficiencies to show what is possible for them.

'It used to be difficult getting children with spina bifida to be independent. They didn't want to know, particularly adolescents – they wanted to forget everything below the waist, so they would get pressure ulcers. They needed to be part of the world. Now they're seen as outpatients, and they live at home.'

In the summer 1975 issue of Heritage News, head occupational therapist Jill Rockey described life in the cottages as 'an experiment in learning by mistakes – by the occupational therapist as well as the school leavers'.

A shopping expedition called for a wide range of decisions: 'How do you get into the greengrocers when you are in a wheelchair and there is a 2in step and the OT is gossiping to a friend down the road? And having got in, there are no cooking apples for your crumble? How do you get things off a high shelf when your arms haven't any power in them? How do you push a trolley when you use crutches?

"The triumph we feel when they solve these problems is enormous.'

Mrs Seymour Obermer, a generous benefactor over many years, presents a prize to Lesley Woolf at the 1975 speech day.

Involving parents was a major new thrust around this time, and one welcomed by Verena Hanbury.

'Having vigilant parents is good,' she says, 'because it keeps everyone on their toes. They want to be very much informed, and as governors we have a duty to keep them informed. Of course there's also a danger of information going out too soon. At a discussion stage, you might discuss something that's worrying for parents to hear, but which is actually never going to come to fruition, so it's important to get information out in the right way at the right time.'

Dr Elizabeth Green joined Chailey in 1981, and remembers that even as recently as that there were fears the Heritage might be closed down.

'About half the children had spina bifida and hydrocephalus,' she says, 'while the others had cerebral palsy and other neurological conditions. I'd first visited the Heritage in the mid 1970s, when I was a post graduate student on a course at Great Ormond Street. I took a demotion in order to work here, because I knew it was what I wanted to do. Things were already changing when I arrived, but the hospital side wasn't quite right: children were placed in their rooms for us to examine them, for instance. This was before the introduction of the Chailey Charter [*page 186*] – children are regarded more as individuals now.

'There hadn't been a doctor at the Heritage with normal school-health skills. Other schoolchildren get immunisation, eye tests and hearing tests simply because they're school pupils, and this was now introduced at Chailey.

'At one time medical conditions which would have been treated in non-disabled children were either overlooked or accepted as an inevitable part of disability. Today it's different. Disabled children are prone to a number of medical conditions, such as hiatus hernia and reflux, which today receive appropriate treatment. Many children with severe cerebral palsy cannot eat and drink sufficient for their needs. In the past these children's growth was stunted, but today their nutritional needs are met by food supplements or alternative ways of eating and drinking.

'In the 1980s most of the children were fairly fit, and some of them never needed medical attention. I went skiing

Consultant orthopaedic surgeon Timothy Morley, who visited Chailey on an honorary basis on Saturday mornings over many years. [Janet Darby]

with them twice as the trip doctor and also to Disneyland in Florida. We were sponsored there by Brighton & Hove Albion and Caledonian Airways.

'Children at Chailey Heritage School today have much more severe neurological conditions and there are far fewer with minor disabilities. We still see those children in our outpatient clinics at Chailey. Few of the pupils at the school today can walk, and many have more severe speech and visual problems. Parents fight to get them to Chailey. Some of those who lose the fight we are able to see as outpatients, which helps a bit.'

And what do parents want for their children at the Heritage? Dr Green, playing devil's advocate, asks whether it might be better to fit the children for their future life outside school by placing the emphasis on language and communication rather than putting them through the national curriculum. Educationalists, on the other hand, favour a multidisciplinary approach, balancing the benefits of curriculum, communication and independence.

The professionals at Chailey have long worked together to ensure the best results for the children in their care, but there's the hint of an old argument here – and of the long-running, historical tension between health and education.

'The visiting consultant staff have provided exceptional services over the years, often in their own time.

'Timothy Morley carried out Saturday morning clinics, performing difficult scoliosis surgery at the Royal National Orthopaedic Hospital, Stanmore.

'Donal Brooks, a world famous hand surgeon, would arrive in his Bentley: he was the most charming person and always discussed problems with the children.

'John Fixsen, a surgeon at Great Ormond Street also gave up his Saturdays – and now David Jones has taken over from him.'

This photograph of Gail Thorne, taken in the orchard at the Old Heritage, appeared on the cover of the spring 1975 issue of Heritage News. [*Tony Tree*]

Education for All

'When I came here in 1984,' says Chailey's headteacher Alistair Bruce, 'I thought I'd walked back in time.'

What he found was a large group of children who had their schooling, not in the main school at the Old Heritage, but in the day rooms of National Health wards at the New Heritage. These were youngsters with more severe physical and learning needs.

'It was still run according to the medical model. The children were here to be treated, and they had some education while that was happening. At a quarter to eleven a trolley came round with drinks and biscuits, and the teacher went off to the staffroom while the nurses looked after the children. I was deputy head, and I was aware of the frustrations experienced by the then headmaster, Hugh Parrott. He knew what he could and couldn't do.

'Back then there were 150 children or so. Funding wasn't an issue: they would just arrive. In fact, it was a cheap option. Health support was given as a matter of course. A consultant at a hospital would have a word with a consultant here, and they'd suddenly appear in class!'

Alistair Bruce admits to engaging in some running battles when he first took over, but change was already well under way. By 1981 long-term admissions of children under four years of age had virtually ceased, and the age profile of Chailey had changed considerably: within a decade the number of children under eight years of age had fallen from 46 per cent of the total to just 16 per cent. In 1974 about a third of the children were at least 50 miles from home, whereas only three years later some 90 per cent of all the Heritage children came from addresses within a 75-mile radius. By 1980, although 55 children went home only for holidays or not at all, a further 45 children were day patients, the same number were weekly boarders and nine were fortnightly boarders.

In the summer of 1984 a working party chaired by Julia Cumberlege was appointed to discuss – yet again, some must surely have murmured – the present and future role of the Heritage. The Warnock Report of 1978 had urged the education of handicapped children in ordinary schools, and the working party was to consider Chailey's role in this context. It was also charged with examining where changes were desirable in order to improve the traditional partnership between the school and the hospital.

By this stage Chailey had become a national centre for the education and care of children with very rare handicaps, such as phocomelia and arthrogryposis, as well as for those dependent on ventilators, and a regional centre for children with spina bifida, Duchenne muscular dystrophy and cerebral palsy. It was also a day school and centre for children from East and West Sussex, Kent and Surrey. Most homes within Chailey's catchment area were no more than two hours travelling time away, and for those unable to go home the Heritage had links with Walsingham House in Hove and Leyden House in Chailey parish, where up to ten children could gain valuable experience of a home environment.

School headmaster Hugh Parrott in Heritage News, autumn 1986: 'Yes, we still await decisions about Chailey's future. We shall still have, dare it be said, an interim report only. The cynics will say "I've heard it all before", and it is wearing to be waiting for decisions which may have an unsettling effect upon not only those of us who work at Chailey, but also those who have a strong affection for its work in the past.

'It is interesting – what rumours have you heard? – to consider whether a cutting down of the number of sites should be viewed as rationalistion or development. We see a single site as a distinct possibility.'

THE CHAILEY NURSERY

Mary Sheppard was a nurse at the Princess Elizabeth Clinic when it closed in the early 1970s because it was felt that babies under two years old should be at home with their families rather than treated in a hospital setting. She left – but very soon found herself called back again.

'I was seconded to Cuckfield Hospital maternity department but had not been there long when Miss Blackmore phoned and asked if I would be willing to set up and run a day nursery in the old PEC building for staff children. She had received several applications from staff who were wanting to work at Chailey but who had dependent children.

'I toured the Heritage, all three sites, and managed to get together tables and chairs, most of which had been put ready to go on the bonfire. Toys were left from the old PEC, and the school provided books, paints and puzzles. Everything had been well used, but was adequate. People were very good and came forward with bits of old carpet and mats, to cover the tiled floor and make it at least look a little warmer, and the sewing room ladies made some curtains. The only new thing we had was a wooden indoor climbing frame.

'For many years we had to make do with being "second-hand Roses", freezing in the cold weather and boiling in the hot, but gradually things took a turn for the better. We had the floor carpeted, and what a difference that made! Gradually more money was allotted for new toys and new outdoor equipment, and many times visitors from other nurseries and hospitals said "What a lovely nursery, and what a lovely situation!".

'From the first summer holiday we started taking young children with special needs from the wards, and it was great to see them with the able-bodied, and learning from each other. In 1980 we officially became a nursery for special needs/able bodies, and Dr McCarthy started sending some very sick and frail little ones. It was good for the parents, who felt that if their children were coming to a nursery with fit, able children, then life couldn't be all that bad.'

A resourceful toddler at play. The nursery was later incorporated with the pre-school assessment unit on the Old Heritage site. [Publicity Designs]

In October 1986 the working party produced its report: *Chailey Heritage: The Way Ahead.* Acknowledging that there had already been a welter of research and reports in the past, it felt that 'despite, or perhaps because of, the volumes written there has been a failure to get through to policy makers and the community. Few seem to appreciate that there is a new philosophy which permeates the Heritage.'

An introduction explained that although the buildings at the Heritage were under the ownership of the Secretary of State for Health and Social Services, the school buildings were leased by the school governors until the year 2009. All children at the Heritage were sponsored by their local education authorities (or in certain cases by social services), which were charged tuition fees decided by the governing body: these fees provided the bulk of the school's income.

'Chailey's dual identities of hospital and school,' began the section on the Heritage's present and future role, 'can easily lead to the misconception that some children are here for medical reasons.' In fact, it emphasised, the assessment procedure for children admitted to Chailey had, under the terms of the 1981 Education Act, to be observed 'according to the educational model'. This involved 'many or all of the following: family doctor, health visitor, social worker, educational welfare officer, educational psychologist, inspectors and advisers in special education, medical consultants, school medical officers, teachers, hospital staff, voluntary agencies, members of the child guidance clinics and, most importantly, the child's parents'.

Not surprisingly, perhaps, the working party recommended that Chailey should continue to provide highly specialised services for rare, severe and multiply-handicapped children, chiefly from the local area, adding that the

From the Way Ahead report, October 1986: 'We have tried to approach our task objectively, conscious of our responsibility to determine whether, in the light of current philosophy, there is any role at all for Chailey to play in the future, and if there is, exactly what that role should be.

'After much thought, research and discussion we are confident that there is such a role; that it is vital in providing for the educational, health and general developmental needs of severely physically handicapped children, and that it is compatible with the recommendations of the 1978 Warnock Report.'

PCs are now an essential tool for most Chailey pupils. [James Luscombe]

Headteacher Alistair Bruce and a happy group of children. [*Daily Mirror*]

From the Way Ahead report: 'Historically the only reason for siting the New Heritage at a distance from the Old Heritage was in order to separate girls from boys. That reason has long since ceased to have any relevance.

'It goes almost without saying that a single site would lead to improved operational efficiency.'

departments of health and education should both be urged to consider Chailey as the model of comprehensive provision for these kinds of children, with a view to establishing similar centres in other parts of the country.

'When I first heard Verena Hanbury talking about Chailey's uniqueness, I bristled,' confesses Alistair Bruce. 'But it's true!

'Over the past century we've always gone with the flow. We've asked "What needs doing that isn't being done elsewhere?" We're presented with a huge challenge today. When I first came here many of the children were taking GCEs, and there was a CSE class, too – because some of them couldn't manage GCEs! Now the great majority have cerebral palsy, with a range of problems: visual impairment, epilepsy, physical and hearing problems. Most have little or no control of their arms and legs, but perhaps some head control. There is often no recognisable verbal communication. They're totally dependent upon adults for care, and this limited independence presents enormous challenges.

'But we've moved beyond the medical model. It's recognised that the children are here to be educated. They deserve the chance to learn. While they are learning we keep going, we keep pouring resources in. They *do* learn. You'll never measure it in outputs. You measure it in terms of what it gives the child in making choices; self advocacy; choosing how to live their lives; learning when they're in danger and when they're safe; who to trust; and how to alert people to their needs.

'Some 14-year-olds might be working at a 3-year-old level cognitively, but they can be excellent communicators – it's great when they're naughty. They make relationships with their peers, and they'll let you know what they want. A child may say "I'm eleven: I don't want baby songs in assembly".

'They can use computers to produce work and to enjoy play, and we use speech systems to help them communicate. Education is also about social skills, and you have to strike the right balance.

'Don't forget that many of our children have average or above average intelligence. Because many aren't able to talk, it's often assumed that they have serious learning disabilities, but it's vital not to underestimate them. They mustn't be written off.'

Funding is not the simple business it was when Alistair Bruce first arrived, and Chailey's work is necessarily expensive. To give a child a 'voice', for instance, costs £5,000, while specialist baths cost around £4,000, hoists £3,000 and armchairs £1,000. The *Way Ahead* report expressed concern that local education authorities might not offer continued support, especially if, under 'pressure from the Department of Education and Science', they made greater provision for severely handicapped children in their own schools.

In the event the LEAs continued to recognise Chailey's special qualities, but the Heritage was faced with meeting the considerable financial implications of another recommendation in the *Way Ahead* report – that it should dispose of its sites at the New Heritage, St George's and Warren Wood, and concentrate all its work at the Old Heritage.

One argument for the one-site recommendation was the sheer logistic difficulty of transporting children from three widely separated locations. Specially adapted buses with rear hydraulic lifts to accommodate wheelchairs (often provided by charities) constantly ran between the different locations. Considerable reorganisation was required to ensure that children were at the pick-up points to meet the buses, and sometimes children would be left at the wrong place: in these cases it wasn't unknown for staff somehow to fit child, callipers and even wheelchairs into their own cars for the short trip to the required destination – so avoiding tears from the children and frustration for the staff at the other end.

The buses were also used for many of the outings arranged for the children (to the seaside and to events such as the South of England Show at Ardingly), and three full-time drivers were required to provide the service. Rationalising the Heritage on one site would certainly save this expense – but it was a minor consideration compared with the staggering cost of moving everything to the Old Heritage, and improving the facilities at the same time.

From the Way Ahead report: 'The working party is conscious that there has been much research, and many reports have been written about Chailey Heritage. Yet despite, or perhaps because of, the volumes written, there has been a failure to get through to policy makers and the community. Few seem to appreciate that there is a new philosophy which permeates the Heritage.

'Ten years ago parents rightly complained that they were made to feel helpless, since Chailey took over total control of their children's lives. Today, parents are active partners in both the education and care of their children.'

WITH A LITTLE HELP FROM MY FRIENDS

Volunteers have always played an invaluable role at the Heritage. A regular feature of Heritage News was the 'Why I Come' column, brief extracts of which are reproduced below.

'When I started on PEC Ward nine years ago I suppose I felt that I had some altruistic idea that I wanted to help children less fortunate than my own, who were then all of school age and disgustingly healthy. Now I have, to a certain extent, changed my mind. The Chailey children may be physically handicapped, but they are happy, and they are becoming people the same as everyone else. Funnily enough, I think it is the happiness of these children themselves that impresses one the most.' (Rosalind Shand)

'I like meeting the parents as well as the children, and feel I can compensate (rather inadequately) for the missing ones by taking some of the children for walks in their wheelchairs. We go and watch the postman collecting letters from the letter box; we chat to the bus driver, no doubt disturbing his forty winks; we go up the lane and talk to the donkey, who answers us sometimes, though in a most unmusical voice! We pick a few wild flowers to take back to Sister, who always accepts them so graciously. Then we go back and change for tea. How we enjoy that cup of tea!' (Nancy Piper)

'By the end of my first afternoon I was utterly bemused, not to say addled, but also completely won over by these children. They are so plucky and such fun. They are naughty and incredibly kind, sometimes unbelievably stupid, and just when you begin to despair of them they switch round and are quite enchanting. I don't know why I come to Chailey, but I think it's really just because I love them all.' (P. Martens)

'Visiting Rennie Ward is not just a visit to a hospital, but a visit to a number of girls who have become real friends and companions. The ward itself is bright and cheerful, with TV and record player, but it is the girls themselves that make it what it is. My first visit was due to a niece of mine who knew of a girl at Rennie, and on visiting us at Newick asked if I could take her to see her. This was fortunately the beginning of a peiod in my life which I am very grateful for, because I am much richer for getting to know the girls of Rennie.' (Anita Wood)

'The work is varied and I am happy to adapt myself to any situation: cutting up the lunch, mixing paint or taking the children out. Visits to the market at Burgess Hill, the post office at Ardingly or shopping sprees can be fraught with incidents, but everyone seems to pull their weight and so ensure the outing is a success. I find even at home that I am collecting material for the play group class, and I think twice before I throw anything away in case it comes in useful for the children. Voluntary work at Chailey is certainly an experience, and I am very grateful to the staff for letting me help them.' (Barbara Hunt)

'It's because of the children, of course. That's why we all come, all the voluntary workers. Not for the children, necessarily, although most of us start out feeling we want to help – our children have grown up, or gone away to school, and we want to do something useful. I come in once a week to Tidemills, and help serve the children's lunches, settle them on their beds for the rest, and then read stories until it is time for them to get up and go to afternoon school. When I first started they played all kinds of tricks, testing me to see how far they could go. Was I soft? Was I strict? Was I fair? Very important this, same treatment for all, and stand in the very centre of the ward when reading. We learn from one another.' (Patricia Tate)

A cruise on the Thames, courtesy of the Variety Club of Great Britain. [Doug McKenzie]

An Ode to Our Gallant Helpers

Heritage teacher Marion Biggs wrote this echo of Kipling
for the autumn 1983 issue of Heritage News

If you can keep your cool when all about you
Are children begging to be taken to the loo;
If you can cope with calipers and standers
And stagger through a visit to the zoo:

If you can bear with temperamental teachers,
Wash paint-pots, flower pots, sticky hands and all,
Thread needles, polish stones and pick up stitches
And stand up heavy youngsters when they fall:

If you have learned to handle Bliss Symbolics
Or wave your arms in Maketonian glee;
If you can do without your morning coffee
And can't find time yourself to have a 'wee':

If you can deal with Fletcher maths and spelling
And in between them fit a leaking patch –
Then Chailey will be proud of your achievements
And you will then have won game, set and match.

A magically impromptu moment during the Queen Mother's 80th anniversary visit in 1983. Young Alex Leaney runs to meet her (inset) and is rewarded with a hand-in-hand walk before the cameras. Also in the photograph, left to right: lady-in-waiting to the Queen Mother Lady Angela Oswald, chairman of the governors J. Rendel Jones, Verena Hanbury and headmaster Hugh Parrott.

The Chailey Challenge

*T*he Heritage had always thrived on the generous donations of its supporters, but the tireless campaigning of the League of Friends, which in 1991 set about raising millions of pounds so that the ambitious *Way Ahead* report might be implemented, can be said to have saved Dame Grace's vision in a manner of which she would have been proud. Indeed, she would have felt very much at home with the list of vice presidents for the so-called Chailey Challenge, including as it did a duchess, a baroness, a marchioness, a lord, two ladies, a knight, a bishop and an admiral.

Although the strategy outlined in the report argued forcibly for all the Heritage facilities to be gathered together on one site, the health authorities remained extremely doubtful as to the suitability of Chailey as the best location for their services. Not only that, but the plans involved a school extension, up to eight children's residential bungalows, a residential medical unit, a replacement swimming pool, riding facilities and an entirely new development centre, including engineering workshops. A million pounds had already been raised for the school extension, but to find funds for the rest of it was a tall order.

Clifford Dann, who was to be the driving force behind the Chailey Challenge (and was chairman of the Friends from 1978–1998), sat on the liaison committee which brought together the school and Brighton Health Authority.

'I well remember the day that we sat down to discuss the feasibility study,' he says, 'and Julia Cumberlege, who was in the chair, announced "This is going to cost £5 million. How will the money be found?".

'I simply replied "The Friends will run an appeal"'.

And so they did, with shrewd planning as much as enthusiasm. In a discussion paper he prepared for the liaison committee in July 1987, Dann wrote 'It is beyond doubt that if the required funds are not forthcoming from private sources, the one-site concept will remain a pipe-dream'. If the League of Friends were to undertake the fund-raising, he added, a professional appeal consultant and a full-time appeal administrator would be essential, as well as an appeals office with a separate telephone.

The Friends, it should be said, had a long record of providing facilities for the Heritage. The organisation was founded in 1954 by C.W. 'Corny' Shelford (then High Sheriff, and a member of numerous Heritage committees over many years) in response to the big question of the 1950s: would the generous donations of its supporters continue after the take-over by central government? The Friends, a registered charity, aimed to maintain relationships with those supporters, to help recruit volunteers and to raise funds for facilities not financed by the state.

The profile of Chailey Heritage was raised through BBC radio's 'This Week's Good Cause' appeals, one given by Godfrey Wynn and another by Ed 'Stewpot' Stewart. The response was incredible, and a team of volunteers would sit at a line of trestle tables opening hundreds of envelopes at a time.

The earliest project was raising £17,000 (a very large sum in those days) for an assembly hall in memory of Dame Grace. Lewes Round Table became involved, and its then secretary, Clifford Dann, joined the Chailey committee. Two major events were put on at the Dripping Pan, Lewes, opened by celebrities – Vera Lynn (now Dame) and the late Jack Train, doyen of the BBC's Twenty Questions. Another great occasion was a preview of the film *The Amorous Prawn*, written and directed by Anthony Kimmins: this took place at the Lewes Odeon Cinema (sadly later demolished), was organised through Round Table and was attended by many celebrities. When the memorial hall was completed in April 1958, it was opened by the Queen Mother.

Over subsequent years the Friends provided a wide range of facilities, including a number of day rooms, two residential units for family use, a shop, recovery ward, major works to Rennie Ward, an occupational therapy unit, special toilet facilities, and a great deal of refurbishment and upgrading. The Louise Barnard swimming pool was built on the hospital site – named after a matron whose wide circle of acquaintances helped raise money for Chailey. These included the author and journalist Nancy Spain, who arranged a feature in *She* magazine, its readers contributing generously towards the original swimming pool and its attractive garden. Margaret Hardy, who worked as a physiotherapist at the Heritage for more than 20 years, recalls how beneficial that pool was, both for recreational and physiotherapy purposes.

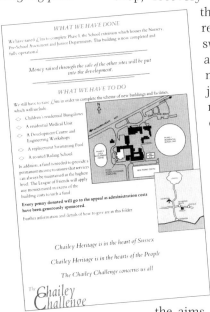

In 1989 the Friends produced a 'How your money has been spent' list covering the previous 35 years, identifying no fewer than 25 major projects and countless smaller ones. There had been a great many fund-raising events, one of the most ambitious being the Heritage Festival (*see p 136*).

The Chailey Challenge, however, was of a very different order. A colour brochure was produced, outlining the aims of the £5 million appeal: 'This development will ensure that physically disabled children and young people will be given even greater opportunities to improve their quality of life and education. It will enable these children to have independent access to all facilities. It will offer independence with safety and independence with choice.'

The scope of the Heritage was explained in similarly pithy terms: 'The centre consists of Chailey Heritage School for over 100 children with severe and complex disabilities; residential care, including 24-hour nursing; clinical consultancy, speech therapy, occupational therapy and physiotherapy, rehabilitation engineering workshops and out-patient facilities.'

And space was also given to 'the Heritage's pioneering spirit', with continuing development including pre-school assessment; day and residential holiday schemes; activity and independence training programmes; and research, development and production of equipment to improve posture, mobility and communication skills.

Dr McCarthy in *Heritage News*, autumn 1991: 'Chailey has always succeeded in responding to change. The next ten years will surely be the most crucial in its history.

'There must be a marriage of minds between the education and health services, an understanding of our symbiotic relationship to produce the most effective services for children.

'The tradition of the past is important for it gives us a foundation on which to build, but it is also important to respond to new ideas which may give new life to the old theme.'

Realising the dream: Friends' chairman Clifford Dann (right) at the Westfield site with John Wells-Thorpe, chairman of the South Downs NHS Trust, and young Timmy Henry, so thrilled to watch the progress of the project that he was declared 'foreman of the works'.

For further details about the Friends and how to join, see page 196.

The Challenge was launched at Buxted Park by the Prime Minister – or so some of the assembled company thought. In fact the guest of honour was Margaret Thatcher's well known impersonator Janet Brown.

'We planned our fund-raising at a time of economic boom,' recalls Clifford Dann, 'but we were in a recession by the time the appeal was launched. It was a critical time. We raised the money in all sorts of ways – through charitable trusts, individual donations and special events. There were sponsored receptions at Newick Park, Horsted Place, the Honorary Artillery Company in London and at St James's Palace – a prestigious event attended by the Queen Mother. We also arranged visits to the Bluebell Railway and to Glyndebourne, an auction at Firle Place . . .'

'Major donations for the clinical services building included £650,000 from one trust and nearly £300,000 from Mrs Cicely Lusted, who some years before had also funded the riding school on the former hospital site. Then for the bungalows and other parts of the project came three donations of £250,000 each, one of £100,000 and, of course, a vast number of smaller donations. The all-weather riding surface near the chapel was largely paid for by one individual sponsor.

'The chief thing was that we raised the money. The Chailey Challenge appeal had been launched in 1991, and it took a little over ten years to reach a successful conclusion.'

And did asking for money Dame Grace-fashion come naturally to Clifford Dann?

'I wasn't quite so direct,' he laughs. 'I gave a fund-raising speech on one occasion and closed it with a memory from my boyhood days at Strict Baptist meetings. I told them that one of the old worthies would always end his prayer "Lord, where I have failed in asking, do Thou make up in giving". I said I would leave that thought with them!'

A good friend: Mrs Cicely Lusted cutting a horseshoe-shaped cake at the opening of the riding school she paid for. Also seen are Pat Wilcox, a Chailey physiotherapist who was for many years in charge of riding for disabled children, and Donal Brooks, a popular visiting consultant. [Janet Darby]

Enterprise

*F*itting disabled children at the Heritage for a job, a major task in the early years, had later come to be seen as a peripheral, even a destructive, consideration at a time when the aspiration was for an all-round education. The pendulum began to swing back when the nature of the disabilities catered for at Chailey meant that few youngsters could hope to sail into the world of work with marketable skills.

At the time of the health service reorganisation of 1974, when the future direction of Chailey was up for debate, headmaster Harry Browning commented: 'We feel there is a need to think about the youngsters who are leaving the Heritage. Not all of them are as easily placed as they used to be. They are more severely handicapped.

'We wonder if there is anything we can do to help them make the transition from school to work, vocational training centre or sheltered placement, and would like to set up an adolescent unit for 16- to 18-year-olds who need to be treated as young adults.'

The emphasis, it should be stressed, was on 'transition' rather than work itself, and this provision was first made outside Chailey. A national survey in 1972 into the employment prospects for adolsescents with spina bifida had suggested that about 20 per cent of them were unlikely to find work.

Made in Chailey: the Enterprise Centre at the Heritage provides work for physically handicapped young men and women – and competes in the market place, too.

At the time, 96 of the 211 children at the Heritage had spina bifida, and a purpose-built unit in West Field was considered, but the principal objection was that it was an isolated rural community with inadequate transport arrangements. (There was also some understandable concern at Chailey that the number of young people attending the centre might be subtracted from the school's allocation of places.)

Various schemes were considered by the Heritage for opening centres in towns such as Brighton, Burgess Hill and Eastbourne, until, in 1978, the Searchlight Workshops Trust (established long before by Miss Muriel Powell, who was formerly a sister at Chailey) made accommodation available at

Among the products made and marketed by the Enterprise Centre: promotional mugs mousemats baseball caps & visors golf umbrellas coasters, wooden and acrylic tote bags placemats teddy bears award plaques safety badges vinyl signs CD clocks acrylic keyrings embroidered labels and badges.

From the Enterprise brochure: 'You name it . . . we print on it! Our process allows us to print onto almost anything . . . aprons, bags, car magnets, workwear, baby clothes, teddy bears, promo gifts, reflectives.'

Anthony House in Newhaven. This offered young people from the ages of 16 to 19 the opportunity to learn skills which would 'develop their potential to live valuable lives as individuals'. This was by no means exclusively aimed at employment (the programmes include educational skills, practical literacy, health education, mobility training, leisure training, 'new experiences' and housecraft), but every effort was made to give the students work experience. After the course some of them moved to specific vocational training, to semi-independent living away from the home or to employment training from home, and Anthony House (named after Dame Grace's son Anthony Kimmins) was regarded as a great success until its closure in 1991.

The elements contained in those programmes are now available in many places, but genuine work experience is a speciality of the Enterprise Centre at Chailey. It was opened in 1995, developed by Graham Barber from his teaching at the Heritage from the 1980s.

'The secondary school was originally organised on traditional lines, with subject teachers,' he explains. 'As disability increased we switched to the primary model – teachers who taught all subjects. When I arrived the craft space was a woodwork room, and all the children were entitled to use it, but as the types of disability changed, the existing equipment was no longer appropriate and we had to introduce workbenches suitable for children in wheelchairs. At first we chiefly used wood, because metal is an unforgiving material, but I later introduced plastic with its bright acrylic colours.

Michael Bylett working on an embroidery program. The spools, seen above his head, are activated by the computer. [James Luscombe]

'Computers started to come in during the mid 1980s, including BBC machines with numeracy and language programs. They brought liberation. By 1988 there was a workstation for each pupil.

Incredible clock . . . the very first product made at the Enterprise Centre.

'In the late 1980s we were invited to join a consortium of non-maintained special schools in East Sussex, under the technical vocational education initiative (TVEI). There was government funding, which allowed us to buy equipment. We moved on to Amstrad computers, which were half the price of the BBC models and could run a range of software that had a 'business' flavour. We explored the usual word processing software, but also used an early graphics design package called Micro Design. This heralded the beginning of our mini enterprise.

'Encouraged to develop mini enterprise as an element of TVEI, we investigated ways in which we could use our developing design skills as a basis for producing marketable products. We finally hit upon the idea of producing images that we could have printed on to the surface of compact discs – the kind used for audio CDs and DVDs today.

'We found a firm in Wales who could print our designs onto the discs. These then had a quartz clock movement mounted on them, and thus was born our first mini enterprise project – The Incredible Clock Company of Chailey.

'In order for us to handle the financial part of the operation, we opened a bank account with Natwest, and received £40 start-up funding. We also received regular business advice from the bank. We sold the clocks to individuals, but there was more mileage in bulk selling, and that gave us the idea of using them as promotional goods.

'Next we bought a badge machine, changed our name to The Incredible Design Company and made button badges. The profits went into our bank account.

'This was all going well, but parents of 15 to 17-year-olds began to ask: "What happens when my child leaves? Sure, they'll go on to a specialist college for two years, but what next?" Early retirement was staring them in the face after that. We're talking, don't forget, about young people with pretty severe physical disabilities and with associated learning difficulties. They had no real chance of getting into the workplace. The best they could hope to be offered would be something menial, such as sticking envelopes, and for many of them their level of motor control was too low for that in any case. To have the curtains suddenly drawn at 19–21 seemed grossly unfair – and immoral.'

During 1992 Graham Barber was given a little time away from Chailey, amounting to about half a day a week, to look into the future. He discovered that the problem was widely recognised that research into it had been going nowhere. Why not, he asked, beef up the mini enterprise

From the Enterprise brochure:

'Colour photocopying: quality colour photocopying up to A3. We can copy on card up to 200gs. Duplexing available.'

'Prints from disk: prints available from disks up to A3 We can copy on card up to 200gsm.'

'Laminating: we can laminate up to A3. Ideal for menus or price lists.'

'Stationery: let us design your stationery, or supply your own artwork and we will print in full colour. Business cards at credit card size, compliment slips and A4 letter-heads. Printed stationery can be used in an ink jet printer.'

'Miscellaneous: artwork and design; greetings cards, binding, ID conference badges.'

project and convert the woodwork room as a workbase rather than a classroom? The Enterprise Centre was born, with Barber as its director, dropping its educational role and providing employment for those who couldn't find it via a traditional route.

'Having made the decision we had to decide on the type of provision we would be offering. Computer technology, obviously, and graphic based. Essays and project work would translate into word processing, and art projects would translate into graphic design.'

It was decided that the project range would be extended, with the young people creating designs for screen printing. Graham Barber put his case to the school governors, and they agreed to underwrite the project for two years. A sum of £30,000 needed to be raised for the refurbishment of the building and purchase of the necessary equipment. In the true spirit of Chailey the money was found, a third of it coming from The Prince's Trust. Just as the project was about to get under way, however, there came a terrible moment of truth.

'It was an absolute 11th hour catastrophe,' recalls Barber. 'On a Monday morning a contractor arrived to continue work with the refurbishment of the premises we were to use. He'd seen the plans, and knew of our intention to make silk screen printing a central process within the Enterprise Centre. An off-the-cuff remark regarding the need for air extraction equipment and solvent recycling ran alarm bells in my head. Was this really a suitable process for us? Neither of these requirements had been pointed out by the suppliers of the silk screen equipment.

'The heaviness of the blow can't be overstated. The whole project seemed to be doomed. The move into garment printing had been seen as a the core element, attracting the orders from customers that in turn would give life and meaning to the work provision we were creating. Without it, a major re-think would need to be done with regard to our business plans. Frankly, I was in despair.

'The young woman who was to have been our first worker at the Enterprise Centre, Michele Hawkes, had mentioned to me some time earlier that a friend of her father was in the colour copying business. That hadn't seemed to be of any use to us at all, and I rang him that evening out of courtesy rather than with any thought that he could help us. Amazingly, it seemed that a copier could do the same job for us as screen printing. Using special transfer paper, images could be produced and printed onto garments using standard colour copying equipment. In addition, the process was hazard-free and well suited to the clean environment we wished to create. By the evening our project had legs again!'

The copier (which interfaced with the centre's computer network) was more expensive than the screen printing equipment, but Barber juggled the accounts. It was leased for £2,000 a quarter, and the Heritage had it on 90 days' lease period, with a renewal required 30 days prior to the expiration of each lease period.

'On one occasion we'd almost reached the 60th day and we were a thousand pounds short. The governors had insisted that the project must be viable, and it wouldn't survive if the copier went. I pored for quite a while over our accounts. Imagine my amazement when I realised I had overlooked a donation of £1,000! We managed to keep going. Now, thank goodness, we have our own colour laser copier.'

Social Services pay for the young people to come to the Enterprise Centre. At the beginning, Barber says, he sensed some doubts about the project, because it was completely new, but demand from the grass roots immediately loosened the purse strings.

'Our next concern was that, under the school's objectives registered with the Charity Commissioners, we could only take on young people up to the age of 25. That would mean the end of the employment road for those who had learned all the skills with us and were putting them to use in their work. The solution was to go it alone – to come out from under the Heritage umbrella and become a separate charitable company.'

Michele Hawkes, here designing badges, was the first worker at the Enterprise Centre.
[James Luscombe]

This bold target was achieved in September 2002 – to the great relief of Michele Hawkes ('Very good – mustard keen!' says Barber), who had by then passed her 25th birthday.

'I first came to Chailey from my primary school in Uckfield,' she says. 'I have Ataxia telangiectasia (AT). I enjoy the design work at the Enterprise Centre very much. It means I've got something to do during the day. If I wasn't here I'd be at home – probably watching telly all day.'

The number of workers like Michele will grow, but the director stresses that the development of the Enterprise Centre has to be managed very carefully. The product range has already increased from printing on T-shirts, with the introduction of a machine to cut vinyls which enables the workforce to produce self-adhesive vinyl signs, and, more recently, new embroidery equipment.

'You could say that we've gone beyond Dame Grace's vision,' says Barber. 'She was fitting young people for work elsewhere, but we're actually providing it here on site.

There are, however, necessary restraints on the business.

'We're here to provide work experience for physically handicapped people and to operate as a viable business, and we have to ensure that these two things are in balance. The work ethic is built into our operation. Everyone is here from 10 until 4, and they all take part in team discussions, and put up ideas for solving problems and creating products. But they of course work relatively slowly, and we mustn't advertise our products so successfully that we can't meet the demand.

'That said, although we certainly don't want to take bread from the mouths of other workers, we do offer quality products, and potential customers may be pleased to know that their purchases promote the valuable work we're doing here rather than paying for a director to have a nice holiday in Barbados!'

A Changing World

Hilary Ford worked at Chailey Heritage from 1965 until 1989, and witnessed many changes in that quarter of a century.

'In 1965 the majority of children had limb deficiences, but this slowly changed, and in their place came children with spina bifida. Also government policy said children should be kept at home for as long as possible, should not be admitted under the age of seven and should not come from long distances.

'We had children from all over the world – children whose families were in the army, based in Gibraltar, Hong Kong and Germany, and English children from the colonies. The army slowly cut down on men who had children with disabilities, as it was inconvenient and expensive to keep them in touch with their families. The policy gradually worked, and most children now had homes to go to.

'So from 1965 when there were 24 children on Christmas Day, by 1989 I would have been amazed to have had any for Christmas or Easter (at least a week at each) and all went for at least two weeks in the summer. There were day scholars, weekly boarders, fortnightly boarders and three-weekly boarders, and that was the longest.

'The number of children with spina bifida slowly began to drop, and children with cerebral palsy and other syndromes took their place. The children with cerebral palsy were often totally dependent and needed a lot of input from the Rehabiliation Engineering Unit. The children with cerebral palsy often came in lying down in an assortment of odd chairs. They were accomodated as soon as was possible in a variety of moulded seating, and later in metal adapted seats which fitted into wheelchairs with a tray on top.

'Most had no speech, so communication was the next problem. Mr Bliss came from the USA to see us, using his Bliss symbols, which were very useful. Then, slowly, communications systems became more and more sophisticated and computerised, and some also included voice boxes. As I left they still had heavy American accents. The children by this time all had invididual moulded toilet seats, and also seats which fitted into both manual and powered wheelchairs and could be lifted onto a car seat or coach seat so that the children could travel easily.

'The change in 23 years was extraordinary. From 24 talking, mobile children, either rolling or walking, then children with spina bifida in calipers walking or standing in standing boxes or pushing a wheelchair around, to nine or 10 totally silent children, all of whom had severe spasms and who needed to be securely seated to enab le them to eat, see properly and concentrate at school.'

All Together Now

At last, in 1998, after years of discussion, planning and fund-raising, all the facilities at Chailey were concentrated on the one site – the Old Heritage where Grace Kimmins had, 95 years previously, brought a handful of brave, poor things to a run-down workhouse.

Many of the buildings she would still have recognised, but there were recent additions which would certainly have surprised her. The school had been extended and several children's residential bungalows had been built in the grounds, while to the south of the site, and with a separate entrance, were the expansive headquarters of the Chailey base of the South Downs Health NHS Trust (successor, since the 1991 NHS Act, to the old Brighton Health District), with all its services under one roof.

Other changes were invisible, including a change of name and a significant change of responsibilities. Gillian McCarthy had explained the former to readers of *Heritage News* in 1990.

'The senior members of staff have been discussing our future for some time,' she wrote. 'Out of these discussion has come the decision to drop the 'Craft School' and 'Hospital' from our title and simply use 'Chailey Heritage', comprising three parts – Chailey Heritage School, Chailey Heritage Child Care Services and Chailey Heritage Rehabilitation and Development Centre. We hope this will give us a sense of common identity whilst explaining our separate specialist areas.'

Today the official titles are Chailey Heritage School and Chailey Heritage NHS Clinical Services.

Clinical Services have academic links with the University of Brighton, University of London, University of Sheffield and with the new Brighton and Sussex Medical School (a partnership between the universities of Brighton and Sussex). They have also collaborated with the NSPCC and the Department of Health concerning the making of training videos and packages.

Books galore: Sam Barkley with classroom assistant Lesley Roots.
[James Luscombe]

The single-site Heritage in the foreground as it is today. The Old Heritage, on the A272, is at the centre of the photograph, with the chapel to the right. On the left, approached from the minor road linking the A272 with the A275, is Westfield, home of Chailey Heritage NHS Clinical Services. The famous windmill can be seen at the top right of the picture next to the former boys' residential block, St George's, now converted to residential apartments. The New Heritage lay half a mile away (some two miles by road) to the north-east.

Angela Jones worked in QEB from 1980 until it closed in 1995.

'The packing up of QEB was a mammoth task, and it was sad, but exciting, when the removal lorry eventually came. We can remember the old building with the rain pouring into the undercover every time we had a downpour; the mice running up and down the corridor at night and frightening the life out of the night staff; the day of the "hurricane", when all the trees blew down, but the building remained intact.'

The presence of mice was explained by Olive Fraser, a nurse in the late 1920s.

'White mice were special pets at the time, and they were kept in cages under the balcony, but they escaped and multiplied so that baby mice kept appearing in the wards at awkward moments.'

The change of responsibilities came in 1996, when the National Health Service felt that it was inappropriate for an NHS trust to be delivering care within a specialist residential school. This meant that the school regained a control of the residential facility at Chailey that had been taken away from it in 1948 – the governors agreeing to this on condition than new residences were built on the Old Heritage site.

Mark Cornwell arrived as bursar less than a year before this sudden withdrawal, and found the move perplexing. 'I was aghast,' he laughs now. 'I'd arrived when there were 72 staff, and suddenly there were 200.'

The health service hadn't gone away, of course, and for headteacher Alistair Bruce this is a tremendous bonus.

'The school has stand-alone status, but having an NHS trust on site is unique. It gives us an edge. There are about 20 broadly similar schools in the country, but none has an NHS presence. Families fight to get their children here. They go to Special Education Needs tribunals and argue for a place. They think we're the best – and so do I.'

Today there are some 26 children boarding for a week or fortnight at a time, plus about 40 at Chailey for some form of respite care, either a day a week or perhaps a fortnight in the holidays. Some two-thirds of the pupils, therefore, use the residential bungalows.

And that age-old tussle between education and health?

'Because the children are here to be educated,' says Alistair Bruce, 'we have the last word. So if the clinical side wanted to see a child at an inappropriate time, I'd say no. But that's hypothetical. Staff relationships are individually very good, so that doesn't arise. There are tensions, of course, but the multi-disciplinary approach produces the best results.'

A so-called 'posture review' for young Ami Ling, deciding what special seating she needs. Her carer, grandmother Ann Ling, is seen second on the right.
[James Luscombe]

Over at Clinical Services, Dr Elizabeth Green wouldn't disagree.

'The relationship between the school and the clinical side is like marriage,' she smiles. 'You have to work at it. But having the school and clinical services on the same site is a wonderful thing: there's nowhere in the world like it.'

As clinical director of paediatric rehabilitation, Dr Green not only works in the posture clinic, sees outpatients and is on after-hours call, but is a consultant in one of the most recent innovations at Chailey, the Children's Head Injury Service.

Dr Elizabeth Green

'This is different from other aspects of our work,' she explains, 'in that we're dealing with children who have had a non-disabled experience of life and then, because of a road accident or severe illness, have suffered brain injury. We have four or five at any one time at Chailey.'

'These children are treated separately from those at the school, because a different approach is needed. They have their own residential accommodation, for instance. These children are often very frustrated, because they've known normal life, but they can improve, and most eventually go back to their own schools.'

Some 130 children and families have received support from the head injury service during the past 15 years.

Valerie Moffat, speech and language therapist at the Heritage since 1992, remembers being with a team which visited 12-year-old Victoria in Cuckfield Hospital after she had been involved in an accident at Chailey crossroads.

'She'd been a bright and intelligent girl who loved singing and playing the cello. Victoria received 18 months of rehabilitation before being integrated into Chailey Heritage School and progressed, as her mother put it, "from a waking coma to relearning certain body movements". She told me that she'd never forget the first time Victoria managed to roll over: "It was such a little thing, but it meant so much."

'This was the beginning of the so-called "rollover rehabilitation" programme, which "rolled" on a daily basis with all the expertise of a multi-professional team and has now been recognised as an important part of the work of Chailey Heritage Clinical Services.'

There are, as Dr Green explains, many separate therapies involved in the clinic, and various teaching strategies, too.

'Some children have lost their memories and some will need to learn to write with their other hand. Some of the children have transferred to the Heritage school, and LEAs will pay for a teacher to come in, as most need a mainstream curriculum.'

Which brings us to the vexed question of hard cash.

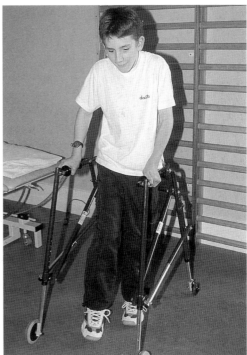

Fourteen-year-old Chris Mason in the gym at the head injury clinic, learning to walk again after an accident. [James Luscombe]

And a proper amount of devilment, no doubt . . .Hannah Hawkins learning through play.
[Daily Mirror]

The Money

Chailey Heritage School has an annual budget of about £3 million, putting it, in the words of bursar Mark Cornwell, 'at the top end of small businesses or at the bottom end of the medium'. It has more than 200 staff, most of them part-time, working round the clock for 48 weeks a year. As it entered the centenary year it was catering for 99 pupils, with tuition and boarding fees paid by local education authorities (LEAs) and respite care in the bungalows met by social services. Each child also gets medical, nursing and therapeutic input from the on-site South Downs NHS Trust, and this is what makes Chailey unique.

Bursar Mark Cornwell – bringing City expertise to the Heritage. [James Luscombe]

'We have a banding system for the LEAs,' explains Mark Cornwell. 'Termly tuition fees, for instance, currently vary from £5,800 for "low needs" to £7,400 for "complex needs", and weekly boarding fees rise from £7,500 per term in band 1 to £10,800 in band 5. You need to ask the right questions in order to assess the appropriate banding and to convince the LEAs that the fees are justified. They've accepted increases of 10 per cent in each of the last two years to keep up with the ever increasing needs of the children.'

The bursar insists that the same financial principles must apply as those he knew in his previous working life in the financial services field. Some 85 per cent of the budget is spent on staff costs in spite of severe scrutiny when extra staff are requested. The school follows national pay scales and, he says, wants to be seen as a good employer – for instance, by offering comprehensive training programmes.

'Getting a place for your child in a non-maintained special school is a long and sometimes complicated procedure,' explains Verena Hanbury. 'This means that it's impossible to be sure of the number of entries for the following year. The only reliable forecast we have is how many are going to leave, and even this is not always accurate, so budgeting is not easy – especially as we have to keep flexible enough to provide for a sudden national need should it occur.

'We have a board of trustees, chaired by Baroness Cumberlege, on which some governors sit. We governors put forward a budget which we hope they will approve – and so far they always have! At the moment our fees haven't kept up with the escalating needs of the children, so we have to "top up" with other income that could be so well spent elswhere. Technology, for example, is racing ahead, opening up exciting opportunities for communication and mobility, but the research and equipment is expensive, and we're always looking for funding to avoid denying the children every chance they've got.

'The local education authorities have to look at our fees as a one-off. If we charge too much the LEAs could try sending the children to their own

Facts and figures:

The annual budget of Chailey Heritage School is in the region of £3,000,000.

85 per cent of expenditure is on staff costs.

There are some 200 part-time staff – the equivalent of about 100 full-time workers.

Fees are paid to Chailey by a child's local education authority for schooling and by his or her local health authority for medical care.

schools. It's not a nice situation when you know that the authorities would rather not use you, although the parents want to use you. Each year we do a zero budgeting exercise so that the fee to the LEAs represents a true cost and can be itemised.

'And there's the medical input as well. Those costs are paid by the child's health authority and charged by the NHS trust. They face the same problem: everyone fights against paying. There's a grey area over equipment. Who pays for it: the school, the LEA, parents or the health authority?'

Chailey Heritage Clinical Services have an annual budget of about £2$\frac{1}{2}$ million, made up from contracts set up with referring health organisations (mostly in London and the south east) and also with funding for 'out of area treatments' for children who come from further away.

'The Trust has been very supportive of Chailey over the years,' says Gillian McCarthy, 'but a major headache has been achieving funding for the expensive services provided. Most children receive tripartite funding: health, education and social services jointly foot the bill.'

'Every time the NHS reorganises,' adds Elizabeth Green, 'and it does so frequently, we're worried that the new funding arrangements will mean that we shall have to reduce our clinical service. So far this hasn't happened.'

The outpatients department at Clinical Services continues to see children with spina bifida, muscular dystrophy and congential conditions of different sorts. Indeed, Chailey is known nationally for its particular expertise in a number of very rare conditions and – just as in Dame Grace's day – it attracts eminent visiting consultants from Great Ormond Street, Guys and the Royal National Orthopaedic Hospital in London.

Unlike the old days, however, is the active involvement of families.

'We have magnificent parents, who are very tough,' says Verena Hanbury. 'Very tough with *me* – but so supportive of their children that it isn't true. It's very good for us to have parents standing up for their rights. Because we're a non-maintained school, the LEAs who pay the fees would much rather send their child to a local authority school which they don't have to pay for – and which they run – than to Chailey Heritage School, where they have to pay what may look like huge fees. If a parent wants a child to come to Chailey the parents will get up and fight.'

Those battles are likely to continue. Although Mark Cornwell insists that the balance sheet is strong, it's clear that the Heritage needs to be as resourceful, as tenacious and as fortunate with its benefactors as at any time in its long history.

Mirror Images

Dame Grace would have been beside herself. Just as, a hundred years before, she had launched her great enterprise with splash stories in the newspapers, so her beloved Heritage approached its centenary with a razzmatazz charity appeal that raised thousands of pounds. Better yet, the newspaper involved was the *Daily Mirror*, which in her heyday had helped raise cash for Chailey through Pip, Squeak and Wilfred and their touring Mirror Grange. Full circle!

The vice-chairman of the school governors, Ian Dipple, had a direct contact with the *Mirror*, since his daughter Jo is on the staff. Another important link was the fact that the *Mirror*'s irrepressible editor, Piers Morgan, was a local lad, who attended a school close by and still has a house in the area. And a third connection: Mr Morgan's home-help, Jenny Allen, also works as a cleaner at the Heritage.

GIVE THESE KIDS A LIFE ran the headline on December 2, 2002, when the paper launched its Christmas appeal.

A report from Jill Palmer, its medical correspondent, explained to readers that some of the pupils were severely brain damaged: 'Most are quadraplegic, few can speak.

'They are totally dependent on others for every physical need. They will never pass any GCSEs, never be able to write with a pen and are unlikely to read a book.

'Yet Chailey heritage School is full of hope and inspiration. It offers a lifeline to its 99 pupils and a daily miracle to their parents.'

Coincidence: the Daily Mirror is celebrating its own centenary in 2003. 'Perhaps we can do something to link the two events,' Piers Morgan has suggested.

There was much more over several days, with large headlines and striking photographs (reproduced on the following pages). As the envelopes poured in, a team of volunteers, six or eight at a time, set about the task of sorting cheques from Gift Aid forms and making sure that every letter was answered. Although the *Mirror* appeal was shared with the Whizz-Kidz charity for non-mobile children, it raised £40,000 for Chailey Heritage School – a major sum that was immediately earmarked for an equipment fund, the emphasis being placed upon new technology.

Above: Ellis Jones in merry mood.

Right: Charlie Baker and his mother out for a ride.

Below: Nicky Loat and swimming assistant in the new pool.

[Daily Mirror]

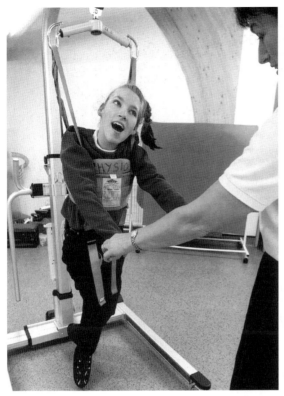

Above: Dannielle Lees with physio Paul Draper.

Above right: Twins Orlanda and Marissa Tasker in Pre-School.

Right: Sam Barkley with Joan Barnes, one of the Heritage lunchtime assistants.

[Daily Mirror]

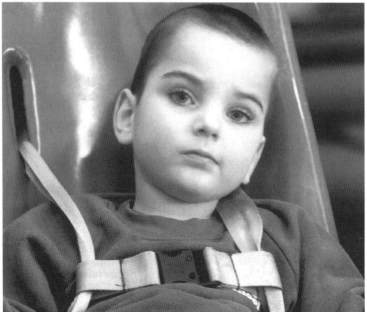

*Above: Andrew Lefroy,
'transport expert'!*

*Left: Bradley Howard in
pensive mood.*

[Daily Mirror]

Right: Kara Warner hard at play.

Below: Becky Linstead with speech and language therapist Nicky Ashdown.

In the pre-school assessment unit, children are offered an early years' curriculum in which they participate in a wide range of early learning activities. Each child has a programme devised by the multi-sensory team and co-ordinated by the teacher. On reaching 5 years old they may join the primary department.

[Daily Mirror]

Ciaron Munday: communication is at the core of the school's work. [*Daily Mirror*]

Today and Tomorrow

One lesson taught by Chailey over the past hundred years is that nothing stands still, and it would surely be unwise to predict the developments of even the next decade with confidence. Headteacher Alistair Bruce certainly feels that 'a huge challenge' faces the Heritage today.

'Previously, change was gradual,' he says, 'but I believe we must make every effort to develop the pioneering provision that we're known for. Children with physical disabilities are quite rightly being educated with increasing success in mainstream provision. With the rapid pace of change today in education, particularly in special education, but also in medical science, the economy and society, our challenge is to make sure that families and local education authorities are aware that they have a choice because of what we provide at Chailey Heritage School. Our aim is that the school continues to be in great demand because of the uniqueness of its provision – a provision acknowledged as unmatched by local mainstream or special schools.

'Perhaps if we were starting afresh with a new school as Dame Grace did a hundred years ago, we'd be considering provision for children within the autistic spectrum as well as those presenting profound learning needs and challenging behaviour: it's an area that seems to be challenging local provision at the moment. But as well as looking ahead, we need to do our very best for the pupils we have here now.

'Demand for places at Chailey Heritage School, in my experience, has never been higher than it is today. That brings its own challenges, with pressures on resources and space, but one of the great advantages of being a non-maintained school is the scope to be self-determining and to be able to make a rigorous response to such a challenge. We have a fantastic team of staff here – dedicated, skilful, energetic – and I feel privileged to lead them in mapping out a very bright future for the school.'

At Chailey Heritage Clinical Services, Dr Elizabeth Green feels that there will always be a demand to care for children with severe disabilities.

'Cerebral palsy is an umbrella term for a number of conditions,' she explains, 'and we'd once hoped that improvements in obstetric and natal care would prevent many of them. We're less sanguine now. It's realised that problems happen much earlier than we thought and in most cases simply aren't preventable.

'The current education model is that all children are educable and should be integrated where possible, and I think that's an area which will come under strong scrutiny.'

Dr Yasmin Khan, clinical director at Chailey, has no doubt that services will continue to evolve.

'Clinicians are usually amazed at the range of expertise and research going on at any one time under one roof,' she says. 'The future lies in developing an expert centre, linked with tertiary NHS centres, university and other academic bodies – both nationally and internationally – in the areas of movement disorders, complex physical disability covering more than

'Chailey Heritage is a wonderful place. It's always managed to meet the needs of the time, from when Grace Kimmins lifted them off the streets, through TB, polio, spina bifida, Thalidomide. It's changed all the time.'

'I criticised the place for its failings, but if I hadn't gone there I wouldn't be where I am today.'

'I am eternally grateful for the fact that they cured me – though sometimes I wonder how, given some of the treatment I and others received!'

'It taught me not to get too uptight about things that you can't change. Also striving to get as much enjoyment out of each day and to recognise when you are happy and savour the moment.'

Verena Hanbury: the founder's granddaughter is chairman of Chailey Heritage School governors in the centenary year.

cerebral palsy, specialist posture and seating services, rehabilitation head injury and applied electronics engineering.

'Our out-patient services should expand significantly to provide specialist medical, therapy and engineering services that aren't easily available elsewhere. Research and education, which has traditionally held a strong place here, will continue to establish evidence for our clinical practice.

'Our link with other neurodisability centres and Royal Colleges will enable us to train post graduate clinicians from other parts of the UK and abroad. Our newly established research department is already moving along these lines. The new NHS guidelines empower us to work with users, and the focus in the future will be greater consultation with our client groups.'

What *is* Chailey Heritage? What's in a name? People are often confused by the side-by-side existence of the school and the health care trust. For Roy Nelham, newly retired director of the rehabilitation services, there's no doubt that it's an all-embracing title.

'Everything on the site is Chailey Heritage,' he says. 'The school, the National Health trust, all the work that's done here. People look at it as a whole when they envisage the Heritage.'

Verena Hanbury, chairman of the school governors and granddaughter of the founder, Grace Kimmins, says those at the school completely agree with this assessment.

'It's the strength of both organisations working together that makes us special and opens our doors to some children who wouldn't otherwise be able to attend school. I'm not a professional, but I'm certain that the Heritage will always be at the sharp end of special education and care.

'Our policy is to provide for children who aren't well provided for elsewhere. That means you take on the more difficult challenges. I should think at the moment we have the biggest group of the most disabled children in the country. The reason that we are more able to cope with that situation than most other places is that we have the NHS presence on site, which means that if their health is bad they have 24 hour cover.'

And what would Grace Kimmins make of the Heritage today?

I ask myself that quite often,' says Verena Hanbury. 'During the 45 years my grandmother gave to realising her dream, she achieved more than most people achieve in a lifetime. Her spirit, her determination, her devotion to the cause were unchallengeable, and the positive message she preached throughout her work remains the foundation upon which we work today. Observance, passion, determination, ruthlessness, charm and pride were the ingredients of her success. She observed the problem, became passionate about it, determined to solve it and was ruthless in her persuasion. Her charm never failed to attract support.

'Her passion was her Heritage; her pride her two sons, Brian and Anthony, and her five grandchildren. I think she'd be chuffed to bits with the way we've moved on. She was never one to look back. I think she wouldn't be at home with the type of child we have here today, because in a way what she excelled at was showing the children off. You don't do that today – it's a different attitude completely. But I think she'd be delighted to know that her original concept was very much alive. She'd also be thrilled to know that her great grandchildren, through their own initiatives, are following in her footsteps and encouraging their generation to give support.

'After her death and the arrival of the health authority my father, Anthony Kimmins, gave as much time as he could to the Heritage, as did many others – Dame Ruth Buckley, Corny Shelford and Gabriel Reed, to name but a few. They were responsible for preserving and taking forward the pioneering spirit on which the place was founded. Today that spirit is as strong and her message as clear as they ever were.

'My forty years at the Heritage have seen dramatic changes – new buildings, different needs, new challenges. We've moved from 200 boys playing football and cricket to a hundred wheelchair users relying on technology to achieve communication and mobility. It's a different world, but it's the one in which we live.

Dame Grace among a group of her boys. [*Hulton Press*]

THE CHAILEY HERITAGE CHARTER

All children and young people linked to Chailey Heritage, wherever they are, whoever they are with, whatever they are doing, have these fundamental rights while in our care:

To be valued as an individual.
To be treated with dignity and respect.
To be cared for as a child first.
To be safe.

Being valued as an individual means:

Being cared for and treated as unique.
Being talked to and about by their own name.
Being consistently cared for across settings.
Being encouraged to be themselves.
Being given enough time to take part, to do things for themselves, to understand and be understood.

Being treated with dignity and respect means:

Being addressed with respect; never referred to or about as if they are their disability, nor as if they are one of their needs, nor as if they are a piece of equipment.
Being involved in conversations; never being talked about as if they are not there.
Having their privacy respected at all times and in all places.
Having all information about them treated carefully, kept safe and shared only with those people who need to know.
Being given the best possible care that can be provided.
Being involved in decisions that affect them: being actively encouraged to express their views and where these cannot be taken into account, then told why.

Being cared for as a child first means:

Having the same rights and choices and as far as possible the same kind of life as other children of their age and culture, taking into account their understanding.
Being given opportunities, help and support to work, to play and to pursue leisure activities.
Being actively supported as part of a family: as far as possible having their parents fully involved in any planning for them and acknowledged as ultimately responsible for them.
Having access to communication equipment at all times, and as far as possible being listened to and heard when they need to communicate, even if it takes a long time. This might mean making a special time later.
Being given information about what is happening before it happens, being given explanations of procedures before they occur.
Gaining knowledge and information about relationships in response to their individual needs.
Being supported to develop self esteem, positive body image and self confidence.
Being helped to understand sexual feelings and behaviour as appropriate to their age and understanding.
Being supported to develop skills such as decision making and assertiveness and an understanding of personal safety.
Being enabled to learn about acceptable and appropriate behaviour and respect for others.
Having their cultural and religious background acknowledged and respected.

Being safe means:

Having the opportunity to take appropriate risks, but not being exposed to unnecessary risks.
Being protected from abuse, whether physical, emotional, sexual or through neglect.
Knowing that they have all of these rights, all of the time they are in the care of Chailey Heritage, and that these rights can only be denied with good cause (ie. if the exercise of the right would be injurious to themselves or others).
Ensuring that all of the important adults in a child's life are aware of these basic rights and being clear about what they can do if these rights are infringed or not respected.

'We have a magnificent staff, both school and NHS, a voluntary workforce second to none and some superb new buildings. On the downside, we still have a frightening amount of money to raise in order to rebuild two of the original buildings, one of which was Dame Grace's home.

'For the future, I hope sincerely that, while there is a need, we shall continue, within our expertise, to fulfil it. My grandmother pioneered education and treatment for disabled children. We must continue that pioneering spirit by keeping abreast of developments and adapting to them.

'Today I see Chailey Heritage School and Chailey Heritage NHS Clinical Services together as an epic production with a cast of a hundred children and a huge supporting company of experts urging each child to become a star. Every production needs an audience, and our sincerest thanks go to our own gallery of loyal and generous supporters who have kept us running for a hundred years.'

Many will imagine the spirit of Dame Grace looking down upon the Heritage's centenary celebrations with immense satisfaction.

'She'd have loved to be here,' says Verena Hanbury, and then adds with a smile, remembering that earlier regime: 'Mind you, I don't think any of today's staff would work for her!'

Heritage Timeline

1903 Foundation of the Heritage for Cripple Boys by Grace Kimmins and Alice Rennie

1908 Foundation of the Llangattock Heritage for Cripple Girls

1911 Foundation of the Boys' Heritage Hospital

Foundation of the Llangattock Craft School for Boys

1912 Foundation of the school chapel of St Martin at the Boys' Heritage

1917 Foundation of the Kitchener Huts, built by the boys so that wounded soldiers might use their own accommodation

Foundation of St Nicholas Home for Raid Shock Children

1918 Foundation of the Botches Home for Raid Shock Children

1922 Sir Jesse Boot's gift provides improved medical and surgical facilities

1923 Erection of the Douty Song School
Erection of the water tower

1924 Foundation of the marine annexe at Tidemills

1925 Erection of war memorial, designed and sculptured by Princess Louise

1931 Foundation of the school chapel of St Helen at the Girls' Heritage

Erection of Pax Est Girl Guide HQ, opened by Lady Baden Powell

1932 Erection of St George's residential block, opened by the Duke of Windsor

Erection of Lily Warren Nurses' Home at Tidemills

1935 Visit of Queen Mary

1936 Opening of the Silver Jubilee Block by the Duchess of York (later Queen and Queen Mother)

1942 Opening by the Duchess of Gloucester of the Queen Elizabeth Home for Blitzed Babes and Toddlers

1943 Opening of 'Liberty', recreation unit for crippled boys at St George's, the gift of the British War Relief Society Incorporated of the United States of America

1945 Visit of the Queen, with Princess Elizabeth and Princess Margaret Rose

1946 Mrs Kimmins writes to the governors, asking to play a less central role in the management of the Heritage

1947 Purchase of two fields (later the Westfield site) from Chailey Parish Council

1948 The Heritage is taken over by the National Health Service. School becomes an independent unit

Gift of Warren Wood by the chairman of governors, Col. J.R. Warren, as additional accommodation for nurses

1950 Dr Philip Quibell joins Chailey as medical administrator

1953 Golden jubilee year

Dr Michael Strode is appointed
resident medical officer

1954 Death of Dame Grace Kimmins

League of Friends formed

1958 Queen Mother opens the Dame Grace
Memorial Hall

1960 First day pupil

1961 Harry Browning succeeds John Broadhurst
as headmaster

1962 Opening of Lady
Hoare Experimental
Workshops by
Princess Margaret

First performance of Nativity Play

1964 Sir Edward Boyle opens new school block

Louise Barnard swimming pool opened
by Lady MacMillan

1969 First edition of *Heritage News*

1972 The Heritage Festival and *son et lumière*

1974 National Health Service reorganised.
House committee disbanded

Reed Cottage is opened on New Heritage
(followed later by Quibell Cottage)

1975 Dr Gillian McCarthy is appointed
consultant paediatrician

1979 Queen Mother visits Chailey

1981 Hugh Parrott becomes headmaster

Dr Elizabeth Green appointed consultant
in paediatric rehabilitation

1983 Queen Mother pays her
final visit, to mark
the Heritage's
80th birthday

1985 Indoor riding school
opened by Lavinia, Duchess of Norfolk

1986 Way Ahead report on the future of
Chailey is published

1991 Chailey Challenge launched by the
Friends of Chailey Heritage

1992 Opening of the Longley building by
the Duchess of Kent

1994 Alistair Bruce appointed headteacher

1995 Opening of residential bungalows by
the Lord Lieutenant of East Sussex,
Admiral Sir Lindsay Bryson

Enterprise Centre opened

1996 Residential responsibility transferred
from the NHS Trust to the school

1997 Opening of the new
swimming pool by Gary
Lineker

1998 Opening of Clinical Services building
by Baroness Cumberlege

1999 First meeting of the Board of Trustees

2000 A group of school children and adults
takes part in Queen Mother's 100th
birthday parade in London

2002 Commemorative plaque to our late Patron
Queen Elizabeth the Queen Mother
is unveiled by Princess Alexandra

2003 Chailey Heritage centenary celebrations

CHAILEY HERITAGE SCHOOL VISION STATEMENT

A That the school continues to be in great demand because of the uniqueness of its provision, a provision acknowledged as unmatched by local mainstream or special schools

B That the school is recognised as a centre of excellence through achieving beacon status from the DfES

C For each pupil to receive all the support necessary for them to reach their individual potential

D For the school to continue to enhance its reputation for innovation in the fields of modern technology and communication, to maximise curriculum access and independence for its pupils

E To have staff that are more knowledgeable, better trained and motivated than staff at any local mainstream or maintained special school

F To offer all staff a working environment in which there is job satisfaction, opportunities for career development, teamwork and the exercise of initiative, so that they may work at all times towards attaining the very best for all the children at the school

G That the school continues to be in the forefront of many educational developments, and recognises that success in all these areas will depend upon the positive contribution of individuals working in cooperation with others to a common goal

H For local education authorities to recognise all these aspects of Chailey Heritage School and to refer children willingly to the school

Who runs Chailey Heritage

1903

PATRON: The Princess Louise, Duchess of Argyll

FOUNDER & HON. SECRETARY: Mrs C.W. Kimmins

TREASURER: Miss Alice Rennie

PRESIDENT AND VISITOR: The Right Hon and Right
Rev the Lord Bishop of London

PATRONESSES:
Duchess of St Albans
Adeline Duchess of Bedford
Countess of Aberdeen
Countess of Antrim
Countess Somers
Countess of Warwick
Lady Moyra Cavendish
Lady Denman
Lady Dickson-Poynder
Lady Jeune
Lady Llangattock
Lady Louise Loder
Lady Henry Somerset
Mrs Cazalet
Mrs Arthur Pearson

THE EXECUTIVE COUNCIL:
Mrs C.W. Kimmins
Mrs Hugh Price Hughes
Miss Alice Rennie
Dr Pawley Bate
Dr C.W. Kimmins
Rev John Scott Lidgett MA, Chairman

THE GENERAL COUNCIL:
Mrs Burgwin
Miss Kathleen Fitzpatrick
Mrs William Garnett
Dr Jane Turnbull
Mrs George Unwin
Mrs Humphry Ward
Colonel R.H. Jelf, R.E.
Sir Cooper Perry
The Right Rev the Lord Bishop of Ripon
The Venerable Archdeacon Wilberforce
Mrs Cecil Chapman

'GUILD CRAFT SCHOOL, THE HERITAGE'
Matron: Miss Stewart
Headmaster: Mr Percy Sykes
Medical Officer: Harold Stevens Basden)
Dental Surgeon: Alfred Mitchell Partridge

2003

PATRON: The Duchess of Gloucester GCVO

SCHOOL TRUSTEES:
The Baroness Cumberlege CBE DL, Chairman
Stephen Hall, Vice chairman
Daniel Briggs
Mark Creamer
Ian Dipple
Mrs Sally Greenwell
Mrs Verena Hanbury DL
Chris Jones
Mrs Jane Roberts
Mrs Charlotte Sharpe
Peter Taylor

SCHOOL GOVERNORS:
Mrs Verena Hanbury DL, Chairman
Ian Dipple, Vice chairman and chairman of finance
Keith Chaplin BSc, PGCE
Dr Elizabeth Green, MD, MBCHB, BA Hons, FRCPCH.DCH
Eric Meadows MA(Ed), BA, MAR, MNFSH
Bill Shelford MA
Peter Taylor RGN. RMN
Mrs Sally Greenwell (West Sussex nominee)
Councillor Joy Waite (East Sussex nominee)
Mrs Chris Russell-Vick (Teacher nominee)
Mrs Joan Martin (Parent nominee)

Headteacher: Alistair Bruce MA

SOUTH DOWNS HEALTH NHS TRUST
Quintin Barry DL, Chairman
Dr Yasmin Khan MD, FRCPCH,
Clinical Director, Chailey Heritage Clinical Services
Dr Charles Fairhurst BSc, MSc, MRCP, MRCPCH,
Consultant neuropaediatrician.
Dr Renate Lipowsky MD, MCRP, MRCPCH,
Consultant neuropaediatrician.

Acknowledgements

Many people have contributed to this book, as is testified by the liberal sprinkling of quotes throughout. It would be easy to take the cooperation of staff and governors for granted, but I should nevertheless like to thank them for responding to my botherings with such good grace. My thanks, too, to former members of staff who not only gave advice and information, but who offered to read first proofs of the book to iron out at least some of my errors and inconsistencies: an inadequate mention here for Janet Darby, Margaret French, Dr Gillian McCarthy, Doreen Quibell, Jill Rockey and Karen Smith.

The response to my appeal in the local press for memories of days gone by was remarkable. The names of many of the people who contacted me appear in these pages, but I am equally grateful to others whose accounts helped to inform my narrative even if I have not used their words directly. My thanks to Susan Adams, Ann Agnew, Carole Armour, David Arnold, Brian Baldock, Elaine Baldock, Michael Baldock, Jean Barnes, Molly Bateson, Brian Bidgood, Rhona Bottomley, Jean Breach, Doris Carter, Heather Couper, Danny Daniels, Margaret Davis, Jose deMontfort, Peter Douch, F.A. Duligall, Marjorie Elphick, Peter Ford, Suzanne Foster, Mrs Franklin, Leslie Garrett, Mrs Grainger, Brian Griffin, Ted Hartwell, Daphne Hewitt, Stephanie Howe, Sheila Jeftha, Lionel Joseph, Kate King, Florence Lamborne, Harriet Lear, Barbara McCabe, Janet McCausland, Eleanor Manvell, Janet Marshall, Tony Medhurst, R. Mitchell, Mrs Parrott, Cynthia Reavell, Anne Ridley, Lawrey Stimpson, Jenny Sutton, Diana Trent, Bernard Trugwell, Jean Tweed, Sylvia Vine, Keith Welton, Angela Wigglesworth, Janet Wilkins, Suzanne Willets, A.J. Williams, Tony Williams, Peter Winstanley and Sonja Wynne.

Photographic Acknowledgements

The Chailey Archive grew randomly, and many of the early photographs lack any indication of who took them. I have given such details wherever possible (in italics), followed by the source of the photograph (in Roman type) if it came from outside the archive. I plead forgiveness for any oversights: the publishers will be pleased to make any necessary amendments in future reprints.

Many of the more recent photographs were taken or supplied by Janet Darby, for years the Heritage's unofficial photographer, and I am especially grateful to her for her help. My thanks, too, to people who offered material from their own collections, including Stephanie Howe, Brenda Izzard and Eric Jenner.

Photographs taken within the months leading up to publication came from two sources. James Luscombe took a series of pictures of various aspects of the work at Chailey, and most are used in the colour sections of the book. Another set of photographs, including the one selected for the front cover, was generously supplied by the *Daily Mirror*, which chose the Heritage as one of two charities to benefit from its 2002 Christmas appeal.

Index

Illustrated entries given in bold

Who Needs Friends?

The first fifty years of this history was centred on the founder, Dame Grace. Progress depended on raising the necessary finance – an aspect on which she was second to none.

With the reorganisation following nationalisation came the need for a voluntary organisation which would work side by side with the school and hospital in helping to maintain the momentum of fund-raising: there would be many facilities which a national government would not be likely to provide. That need was recognised by the then High Sheriff for East Sussex, Mr C.W. ('Corny') Shelford, who had served on numerous Heritage committees and who lived close by. Not only did his vision and drive lead to the establishment of the League of Friends as a registered charity, but he emulated the Dame's knack of getting influential people involved. He was to set a pattern which is still followed.

The team in 1954 included a treasurer, Sir Otto Niemeyer, who had just retired as director of the Bank of England; Lord Moran, past president of the Royal College of Physicians; and James Wilkie, then secretary of the Carnegie UK Trust and also a winner of 'Brain of Britain'. (Clifford Dann recalls his first meeting in the committee when Mr Wilkie remarked about someone who had been upset about something 'Those who mind don't matter, and those who matter don't mind'.)

Of course, royal patronage was sought, and presidents over the years have included the Marchioness of Abergavenny, the Duke of Norfolk, Lavinia Duchess of Norfolk, Mr C.W. Shelford, and now Baroness Cumberlege.

As the years went by others joined the committee – Lady Rupert Nevill, Lady Mary Fitzalan Howard, Lady Creasey, the Hon Dame Ruth Buckley, Lady Dorothy Macmillan, Mrs Ernest Kleinwort, Mrs Winston Churchill, the Hon Mrs Rosalind Shand, Sir William Lindsay, Sir Philip Rogers, Mrs Michael Warren, Mrs Angela Fox and a host of others, all of whom have contributed their time and energy in ensuring the work of the charity would go from success to success.

Little wonder that since its formation the League of Friends (now known simply as The Friends) achieved so much. In the period to 1991 funds were raised for many projects, including:

The Memorial Hall
Occupational therapy unit
Two bungalows for visiting parents
Paddling pools and garden
Recovery room ramp
Upgrading dormitories
Resurfacing playground
The first swimming pool
Prefects' room
Friends' shop
Hairdressing salon
Enlargement of Rennie Ward
Home economics classroom
Greenhouse and potting shed
Various Day rooms
Games room
Hobbies room
Sun parlour
Upgrading of other wards
Secondary school hygiene unit
Caravans for children's use

Since the Chailey Challenge appeal (*see pages 159–162*) support has been given for other projects, including the Enterprise Centre, a research project for powered mobility users and the posture assessment clinic.

It is noticeable that the office of chairman has resulted in long periods of service: Mr Shelford 1954–1965, Mrs Gabriel Reed 1965–1978 and Mr Dann 1978–1998. Now Mrs Ann Jones (whose daughter Jo was a pupil at the Heritage and whose husband Chris was a former treasurer of the Friends) is in the chair.

Enquiries will be welcome from anyone interested in helping in the work of the Friends. Messages may be left at the office on 01825 724472, or addressed to the Friends of Chailey Heritage, North Chailey, Sussex BN8 4EF.